KHUSHWANT SINGH'S BOOK OF
UNFORGETTABLE WOMEN

Khushwant Singh was born in 1915 in Hadali, Punjab. He was educated at Government College, Lahore and at King's College and the Inner Temple in London. He practised at the Lahore High Court for several years before joining the Indian Ministry of External Affairs in 1947. He began a distinguished career as a journalist with All India Radio in 1951. Since then he has been founder-editor of *Yojna* (1951-1953), editor of the *Illustrated Weekly of India* (1979-1980), chief editor of *New Delhi* (1979-1980), and editor of the *Hindustan Times* (1980-1983). Today he is India's best-known columnist and journalist.

Khushwant Singh has also had an extremely successful career as a writer. Among the works he has published are a classic two-volume history of the Sikhs, several novels (the best known of which are *Delhi*, *Train to Pakistan* and *The Company of Women*), and a number of translated works and non-fiction books on Delhi, nature and current affairs.

Khushwant Singh was Member of Parliament from 1980 to 1986. Among other honours he was awarded the Padma Bhushan in 1974 by the President of India (he returned the decoration in 1984 in protest against the Union Government's siege of the Golden Temple, Amritsar).

KHUSHWANT SINGH'S

BOOK OF
unforgettable
WOMEN

Compiled and Edited by Mala Dayal

PENGUIN BOOKS

PENGUIN BOOKS

Published by the Penguin Group

Penguin Books India Pvt. Ltd, 11 Community Centre, Panchsheel Park, New Delhi 110 017, India

Penguin Group (USA) Inc., 375 Hudson Street, New York, New York 10014, USA

Penguin Group (Canada), 90 Eglinton Avenue East, Suite 700, Toronto, Ontario, M4P 2Y3, Canada (a division of Pearson Penguin Canada Inc.)

Penguin Books Ltd, 80 Strand, London WC2R 0RL, England

Penguin Ireland, 25 St Stephen's Green, Dublin 2, Ireland (a division of Penguin Books Ltd)

Penguin Group (Australia), 250 Camberwell Road, Camberwell, Victoria 3124, Australia (a division of Pearson Australia Group Pty Ltd)

Penguin Group (NZ), 67 Apollo Drive, Rosedale, Auckland 0632, New Zealand (a division of Pearson New Zealand Ltd)

Penguin Group (South Africa) (Pty) Ltd, 24 Sturdee Avenue, Rosebank, Johannesburg 2196, South Africa

Penguin Books Ltd, Registered Offices: 80 Strand, London WC2R 0RL, England

First published by Penguin Books India 2000

Copyright © Mala Dayal 2000

18 17 16 15 14 13

ISBN 9780141000862

Grateful acknowledgement is made to the following for permission to include copyright material: Ravi Dayal for 'The Portrait of a Lady', 'Martha Stack' (originally published as 'Black Jasmine'), 'Lady Mohan Lal' (originally published as 'Karma'), 'Bindo' (originally published as 'The Rape'), 'Jean Memsahib' (originally published as 'The Memsahib of Mandla'), 'Nooran' (from *Train to Pakistan*), 'Beena' and 'Champak' (from *I Shall Not Hear the Nightingale*); Mala Dayal for 'The Women of India' and 'Sex in Indian Life'.

Typeset in Casablanca by SÜRYA, New Delhi
Printed at Akash Press, New Delhi

Contents

The Portrait of A Lady

My grandmother, like everybody's grandmother, was an old woman. She had been old and wrinkled for the twenty years that I had known her. People said that she had once been young and pretty and had even had a husband, but that was hard to believe. My grandfather's portrait hung above the mantelpiece in the drawing room. He wore a big turban and loose-fitting clothes. His long white beard covered the best part of his chest and he looked at least a hundred years old. He did not look the sort of person who would have a wife or children. He looked as if he could only have lots and lots of grandchildren. As for my grandmother being young and pretty, the thought was almost revolting. She often told us of the games she used to play as a child. That seemed quite absurd and undignified on her part and we treated it like the tales of the prophets she used to tell us.

She had always been short and fat and slightly bent. Her face was a crisscross of wrinkles running from everywhere to everywhere. No, we were certain she had always been as we had known her. Old, so terribly old that she could not have grown older, and had stayed at the same age for twenty years. She could never have been pretty; but she was always beautiful. She hobbled about the house in spotless white with one hand resting on her waist to balance her stoop and the other telling the beads of her rosary. Her silver locks were scattered untidily over her pale, puckered face, and her lips constantly moved in inaudible prayer. Yes, she was beautiful. She was like the winter landscape in the mountains, an expanse of pure white serenity breathing peace and contentment.

My grandmother and I were good friends. My parents left me with her when they went to live in the city and we were constantly together. She used to wake me up in the morning and get me ready for school. She said her morning prayer in a monotonous sing-song while she bathed and dressed me in the hope that I would listen and get to know it by heart. I listened because I loved her voice but never bothered to learn it. Then she would fetch my wooden slate which she had already washed and plastered with yellow chalk, a tiny earthen ink pot and a reed pen, tie them all in a bundle and hand it to me. After a breakfast of a thick, stale chapatti with a little butter and sugar spread on it, we went to school. She carried several stale chapattis with her for the village dogs.

My grandmother always went to school with me because the school was attached to the temple. The priest taught us the alphabet and the morning prayer. While the children sat in rows on either side of the veranda singing the alphabet or the prayer in a chorus, my grandmother sat inside reading the scriptures. When we had both finished, we would walk back together. This time the village dogs would meet us at the temple door. They followed us to our home growling and fighting each other for the chapattis we threw to them.

When my parents were comfortably settled in the city, they sent for us. That was a turning point in our friendship. Although we shared the same room, my grandmother no longer came to school with me. I used to go to an English school in a motor bus. There were no dogs in the streets and she took to feeding sparrows in the courtyard of our city house.

As the years rolled by we saw less of each other. For some time she continued to wake me up and get me ready for school. When I came back she would ask me what the teacher had taught me. I would tell her English words and little things of western science and learning, the law of gravity, Archimedes' principle, the world being round, etc. This made her unhappy. She could not help me with my lessons. She did not believe in the things they taught at the English school and was distressed that there was no teaching about God and the scriptures. One day I announced that we were being given music lessons. She was very disturbed. To her, music had lewd associations. It was the monopoly of harlots and beggars and not meant for gentle folk. She rarely talked to me after that.

When I went up to University, I was given a room of my own. The common link of friendship was snapped. My grandmother accepted her seclusion with resignation. She rarely left her spinning wheel to talk to anyone. From sunrise to sunset she sat by her wheel spinning and reciting prayers. Only in the afternoon she relaxed for a while to feed the sparrows. While she sat in the veranda breaking the bread into little bits, hundreds of little birds collected around her creating a veritable bedlam of chirrupings. Some came and perched on her legs, others on her shoulders. Some even sat on her head. She smiled but never shoo'd them away. It used to be the happiest half-hour of the day for her.

When I decided to go abroad for further studies, I was sure my grandmother would be upset. I would be away for five years, and at her age, one could never tell. But my grandmother could. She was not even sentimental. She came to see me off at the railway station but did not talk or show any emotion. Her lips moved in prayer, her mind was lost in prayer. Her fingers were busy telling the beads of her rosary. Silently she kissed my forehead, and when I left I cherished the moist imprint as perhaps the last sign of physical contact between us.

But that was not so. After five years I came back home and was met by her at the station. She did not look a day older. She still had no time for words, and while she clasped me in her arms I could hear her reciting her prayer. Even on the first day of my arrival, her happiest moments were with her sparrows whom she fed longer and with frivolous rebukes.

In the evening a change came over her. She did not pray. She collected the women of the neighbourhood, got an old drum and started to sing. For several hours she thumped the sagging skins of the dilapidated drum and sang of the homecoming of warriors. We had to persuade her to stop, to avoid overstraining. That was the first time since I had known her that she did not pray.

The next morning she was taken ill. It was a mild fever and the doctor told us that it would go. But my grandmother thought differently. She told us that her end was near. She said that since only a few hours before the close of the last chapter of her life she had omitted to pray, she was not going to waste any more time talking to us.

We protested. But she ignored our protests. She lay peacefully in bed praying and telling her beads. Even before we could suspect, her lips stopped moving and the rosary fell from her lifeless fingers. A peaceful pallor spread on her face and we knew that she was dead.

We lifted her off the bed and, as is customary, laid her on the ground and covered her with a red shroud. After a few hours of mourning we left her alone to make arrangements for her funeral.

In the evening we went to her room with a crude stretcher to take her to be cremated. The sun was setting and had lit her room and veranda with a blaze of golden light. We stopped halfway in the courtyard. All over the veranda and in her room right up to where she lay dead and stiff wrapped in the red shroud, thousands of sparrows sat scattered on the floor. There was no chirping. We felt sorry for the birds and my mother fetched some bread for them. She broke it into little crumbs, the way my grandmother used to, and threw it to them. The sparrows took no notice of the bread. When we carried my grandmother's corpse off, they flew away quietly. Next morning the sweeper swept the bread crumbs into the dustbin.

The Women of India

'How can a woman rule this country?' demanded my seventy-five-year-old father as he heard the announcement that Mrs Gandhi's election as prime minister of India was assured.

The entire family—my aged parents, my brothers, their wives and children, mostly teenagers at school or college—had gathered for lunch. The news about Indira Gandhi came on the air while we were having coffee.

'Can a woman rule a country like India?' my father asked again, switching off the radio to emphasize the gravity of the problem. None of the grown-ups took up the challenge. A few of the girls, in ponytails and jeans, began to giggle; thinking the elders weren't looking, they shook hands and gave the boys the thumbs-down sign. The boys retaliated by thumbing their noses. Suddenly the giggling and gesturing froze under my father's stern gaze. 'The country will be ruined,' he declared with authority.

It is bad form to contradict the head of the family directly. But there are subtle ways of doing it. 'What choice do we have in the matter?' asked one of my brothers.

'Any one of the others would be better than her,' roared my father. 'She's being put there because she is Nehru's daughter. What kind of democracy is this?' My father did not admire Nehru. But his line of argument was soon demolished: Nehru had been succeeded by Shastri, not by his daughter. We then considered the alternatives.

Morarji Desai? He was all for prohibition and the compulsory teaching of Hindi. He was a strong man but also a faddist. Didn't he recommend drinking cow's urine for health, to a visiting statesman? And didn't he publicly boast of having had no sex with his wife for the last twenty-five years? No, definitely not Morarji Desai.

What about Gulzari Lal Nanda—with those holy men and yogis in saffron around him all the time? He hardly made a decision without first consulting horoscopists and soothsayers. Good administrator and a good standby . . . like the spare wheel of a car. *Arthi mantri* (the pall-bearer minister), they rightly called him! Good enough to be No. 2; prime minister, no.

Kumaraswami Kamaraj? Nice, comforting

father figure and a shrewd, honest politician. But can't speak Hindi or English. Perhaps some day when he had learned one language or the other.

Defence Minister Y.B. Chavan? Politician S.K. Patil? Neither of them as a national figure yet. But they might become so in another few years.

So who were we left with? Indira Gandhi. By then we felt we had been mean to her and a few grudging tributes were pieced together: 'She is better educated than the others and more sophisticated . . . She will be able to talk to people like Johnson and Kosygin and Wilson and De Gaulle . . . She knows how to behave properly and she can be a great charmer when she wants to be . . . She is undoubtedly good-looking. Didn't someone say he would like Indira to be prime minister if for no other reason than to look at a pretty face in the newspapers every morning? And she has a very appropriate middle name, Priyadarshini (of comely appearance) . . . She is not a good administrator—what did she make of the ministry of information and broadcasting when she headed it—but she can leave that kind of thing to civil servants.

We have no choice; it has to be Indira Gandhi.'

My father conceded the argument all along the line. But though vanquished, he continued to grumble. 'Mark my words, we are heading towards disaster. No woman can possibly rule a country like India.'

Ours is an Anglicized upper-middle-class family in New Delhi. As numbers go, the Anglicized upper class is very small. But the vast majority of senior civil servants, politicians and opinion-makers come from it.

It is from this class that every one of India's women leaders was and is drawn: the poetess Sarojini Naidu ('Love to all and a kiss to the new soul of India,' she wrote to Nehru on the birth of Indira) and her daughter Padmaja, who was governor of West Bengal; the painter Amrita Shergil; Rajkumari Amrit Kaur, first woman in Nehru's cabinet; the family planner Dhanvanthi Rama Rau and her daughter, the author Santha Rama Rau; Mrs Vijayalakshmi Pandit, first and only woman to be President of the United Nations General Assembly, and her novelist daughter Nayantara; Sucheta Kripalani, chief minister of Uttar Pradesh; Kamaladevi Chattopadhyay, chairman of the All India Handicrafts Board;

the beautiful maharanis and begums elected to the Lok Sabha (Parliament) and the state legislatures.

There is no such thing as a working-class woman leader in India. At any women's conference, the accents of Oxford, Cambridge, Vassar and Smith and the chi chi sing-song of the girls' schools run by European or American nuns come through distinctly. The granting of equal rights to women who are far from being the social or educational equals of men has brought a bumper harvest of important positions to the very small number of women who are capable of grasping the opportunity.

The visitors' gallery of the Lok Sabha is a good place to get a bird's-eye view of the new ruling class. Once when I went there, the difference between the men and women members of the House was remarkable. While men came from all classes, ranging from the dapperly-dressed 'wogs', tradesmen wearing dhotis, trade unionists in open collars, and sparsely-clad tribesmen sitting cross-legged on the benches, all the women (I counted forty in the hall) were well-dressed; it was obvious they came from the upper crust of Indian society.

Some women were on the Government benches alongside Prime Minister Nehru: Dr Sushila Nayar, minister of health; Mrs Lakshmi Menon, deputy minister of external affairs and the deputy minister of finance; the fair, buxom Tarakeshwari Sinha whose raven-black kiss-curl dangled on a cheek. (An American Senator introduced to Mrs Sinha was so overcome that all he could stutter was: 'You are the most beautiful woman deputy finance minister I have ever met.')

On the opposition benches, outshining other women parliamentarians, was Gayatri Devi, Maharani of Jaipur and a member of the conservative Swatantra Party. At that moment she was needling Nehru on his foreign policy. The prime minister, who had encouraged women to enter politics, was hoist on his own petard. 'I will not bandy words with a lady,' he said, somewhat exasperated.

I saw the Maharani twice again that day; first, at a private party where Jayaprakash Narayan, the pacifist leader, was giving an informal briefing on the negotiations with hostile Naga tribesmen fighting for independence from India. The meeting had begun when the Maharani made her entry, giving everyone a whiff of expensive French perfume. She was dressed in a turquoise-blue chiffon sari with silver sequins sparkling like stars on a moonless night. She looked around with her large almond eyes. Everyone stood up. As Hilaire Belloc once described someone, 'her face was like the king's command when all the swords are drawn.'

She murmured an apology for being late, brushed the hair off her face, asked everyone to sit down and gracefully sank down on the carpet. 'This is indeed a revolution,' remarked Narayan, 'a maharani sitting at the feet of the commoners!' The Maharani replied with a charming smile. She took out a gold case from her handbag and lit a mauve-coloured cigarette.

At the end of the briefing she asked a few questions in impeccable English. Her Hindustani, in which she had argued with some people in the room, was not so good. 'My mother tongue is Bengali and I am married to a Rajput,' she explained. A man sitting next to me leaned over and whispered in my ear, 'Her Bengali and Rajasthani are worse than her Hindustani. She can only speak English and French.'

I saw the Maharani again later that
evening at a cocktail dance at the exclusive
Gymkhana Club. She was with her husband
and his son. The Prince was in military
uniform and spent more time doing the twist
on the floor than with his father's party. The
Maharajah and Maharani remained at their
table drinking French champagne (Rs 245 a
bottle). The Maharajah did not sign the bill
for it; it was the gift of erstwhile subjects and
admirers.

Gayatri Devi is a princess in her own
right; she belongs to the house of Cooch
Behar, famous for producing the hardest
drinking men and most exquisitely lovely
princesses. When she married the Maharajah
of Jaipur, he already had two wives with
children living. Despite her education and
emancipation, Gayatri Devi agreed to be his
third wife because polygamy was accepted by
tradition in the princely order. To this day
many princes have many wives; the late Nizam
of Hyderabad maintained a harem of several
hundred begums and concubines.

When ruling powers were taken away
from the princes and their estates were
reduced to modest proportions, many princes

went into business. The Jaipurs, although still
enormously wealthy, converted one of their
palaces into a hotel and begin to organize
tiger hunts for rich Americans. Gayatri Devi
joined the Swatantra Party, trounced the
Congress party candidate in the election and
became a thorn in the side of Nehru's
Government. Shastri very wisely made her
husband Ambassador to Spain, hoping to be
rid of Gayatri Devi at the next election. But
the Maharani is very much on the scene. She
is today the most powerful woman leader in
the state of Rajasthan in north-west India.

Between the cities of India and its 550,000
villages, and between its elegant, educated
ladies who grace the Lok Sabha and the vast
majority of Indian women, yawns the gulf of
many centuries. The lives of these women
have not changed very much with the passage
of time. Those whose mothers and
grandmothers always enjoyed a certain degree
of liberty still enjoy it today. Women of
southern India, Kerala for example, are more
advanced than women in other parts of India
because regional matriarchal traditions remain
prevalent. In general, women of the lower
castes and income groups have greater

freedom than higher-caste, middle-income women—as they have had in the past. And those whose female ancestors were cloistered in the zenana—women's apartments—still remain cloistered in the zenana. Though the Constitution Act of 1949 guaranteed women legal equality, they are still subject to humiliating extra-legal restrictions.

Yet the lot of Indian women has not always been hard and subservient. On the contrary, our early pre-Aryan female ancestors enjoyed a license that would shock the avant-garde of today. They wore nothing above the waist and the barest minimum below it. They drank strong liquor, danced till the early hours of the morning and were not inhibited in their sexual relations. It was more common for a woman to have four or five husbands than for a man to have a harem of women. They owned property because the society was matriarchal. Today in India, these poor, illiterate, jungle-dwelling Adivasis number about thirty-five million. Traces of their way of life can still be found among the aboriginal tribes in the hills and jungles stretching from Assam in the north-east to Cape Comorin in the south, as well as among the Dravidians in the south.

Aryans, who started coming to India around 3,000 BC accepted this pattern of life at first. In their great Sanskrit epic, the *Mahabharata*, a king unable to impregnate his queen persuades her to seek the services of other men as sanctioned by ancient tradition: 'Women in olden days were not immured within their houses, nor were they dependent on their husbands and yet they were not considered sinful; for that was the sanctioned custom of the age.'

In this state of affairs the notion of paternity was of little importance; bastardy carried no stigma. 'Attending on an honoured guest' was enjoined as a part of hospitality. This freedom continued up to the period of the *Rig Veda* (circa 1500 BC), which refers to women as equals of men, participating in debates, in the performance of religious rituals and in the pleasures of wine and the flesh.

The change in female status came soon afterward. First, polyandrous intercourse was stopped. Pronounced the sage Uddalaka Swetaketu: 'One woman can make love to one man only . . . If a woman is unfaithful to her husband, from today onward it will be a sin.'

Then followed denigration of the woman to a mere producer of children—like a field producing crops. If she bore sons, she was partly redeemed; but if she had daughters, she could be legitimately cast aside and her female offspring destroyed as weeds. Woman became unclean ('Below her navel a woman is always unclean,' says the *Atharva Veda*) and an instrument of the devil to tempt good men to stray from the path of righteousness. According to the *Maitreyani Samhita*, 'Woman is on a par with dice and drink, a major social evil, the spirit of untruth, the genius of darkness.'

The chief apologist for lowering the status of women was the famous lawgiver Manu— also the father of the Hindu caste system— who lived around 200 BC. 'Woman is as foul as falsehood itself,' he wrote. 'When creating them, the lord of creatures allotted to women a love of their beds, of their seat and ornaments; impure thoughts, wrath, dishonesty, malice and bad conduct.' Manu emphasized woman's secondary role in life. 'From the cradle to the grave a woman is dependent on a male: in childhood on her father, in youth on her husband, in old age on her son.'

Manu prescribed early marriage—between the ages of eight and ten for girls—and pronounced a curse on parents in whose home an unmarried girl attained puberty. He also declared that a married woman could own no property. 'Three persons—a wife, a son and a slave—are declared by law to have no wealth exclusively their own. Their wealth belongs to whom they belong.'

Manu was also responsible for the deification of the husband. 'Whether a drunkard, leper, sadist or wife-beater, a husband is to be worshipped as God,' he wrote. The husband-God concept caught on. 'Having offered adoration to the mind-born divinity, let the wife worship her husband with ornaments, flowers and raiment, thinking all the time, "This is the God of love" ', states a religious work.

Sati—the immolation of widows on the funeral pyre of the husband—was the next logical downward-step women were forced to take.

Gautama Buddha, in the fifth century BC, disapproved of child marriage and sati but did little to ameliorate the sorry state of Indian womanhood. Buddhist emphasis on celibacy made woman appear as the seducer of good men. 'Do not see womankind,' enjoined the Buddha.

'But if we see women, what are we to do?' asked his chief disciple.

'Abstain from speech.'

'But if they speak to us, then what are we to do?' persisted the disciple.

'Keep wide awake,' warned the Wise One.

By the beginning of the Christian era, the practice of destroying female children at birth, infant marriage, polygamy, prostitution, mass burning of widows on defeat in war—all this had become common, with the sanction of Hindu religion.

And worse was yet to come. Muslims began invading India about 1000 AD and ruled large parts of the country for the next 700 years. Although Islamic law entitled a woman to own property and to divorce her husband, most Hindus who were converted to Islam continued to observe their own customs: property and divorce remained the prerogative of the male. Muslims also introduced the institution of purdah, the veil, and seclusion of women in harems. Hindus of the upper classes imitated the Muslim rulers by incarcerating their women in the zenana.

The poorer classes treated widows as an abomination. Their heads were shaved, they were not allowed to wear jewellery and could dress only in the plainest white. Even the sight of a widow was believed to bring bad luck. Many were forced into beggary or prostitution either in brothels or attached to temples as devadasis (servants of the Lord). To this day, the Hindustani word for a widow and a prostitute is the same: *raand*.

Change for the better came with British rule. A small band of enlightened Indians supported the British reformers against orthodox Hindu reactionaries. In 1829, the viceroy, Lord William Bentinck, outlawed sati. His chief supporter was Rammohan Roy, who had seen his own brother's widow forced onto her husband's funeral pyre. Remarriage of widows was legalized in 1856. And it was as late as 1929 that a law was passed prohibiting the marriage of children.

The big breakthrough came in the 1920s under the inspired leadership of Mahatma Gandhi. Women by the thousands joined the passive resistance movement, including many women leaders of today—and one of them was, of course, Indira Gandhi. Education was given top priority. Two reformers, the Theosophist Annie Besant and Margaret Cousins, were responsible for founding many women's organizations of which the most active today are the All India Women's Conference and the Federation of University Women.

Nehru carried the process of women's emancipation to its current stage, against the wishes of the majority of Hindus. More than anyone else, he was responsible for the Constitution Act of 1949 which guarantees that 'the state shall not discriminate against any citizen on grounds of race, caste, sex, place of birth'. In 1955 polygamy was outlawed, and after 2,000 years, the right of divorce was restored to Hindu women. In 1956 Hindu women were given equal property rights.

Nehru also pressed women into political life. By law, every village council must have a woman member. The Congress party and following its lead, the opposition parties, set up a quota of women candidates for election. In the last general election, forty per cent of the 100 million eligible women voters cast their ballots. Today there are fifty-nine women in the Indian Parliament (compared with twelve in the United States Congress) and 195 in the state legislatures.

India has more women in important positions than any other country in the world. But it would be wrong to deduce that the women in India are more emancipated than women of other countries. Except in the top layers of society, the pattern has not changed very much and fewer than ten per cent of Indian women can read or write.

Among minority communities, Parsi women are almost European in their way of life. Christians (twelve million) and Sikhs (eight million) have not inherited anti-feminist traditions; their women are more educated than Hindu women and are better represented, for example, in the nursing and teaching professions.

It is different with India's fifty million Muslims. The plight of the Muslim women is worse than their Hindu counterparts.

Bhopal, in the heart of India, is a Muslim city in the midst of a predominantly Hindu state. And since many well-to-do Muslim families have migrated to Pakistan, those who remain are desperately poor and dejected.

The streets of Bhopal are full of beggars.
Lepers dig their stumps into your ribs, crying,
'In the name of Allah!' Women in dirty
burkhas—head-to-toe costumes with holes cut
for eyes—slide alongside like apparitions and
whine, 'In the name of Allah!' Pimps with
long hair and black antimony in their eyes
(used both cosmetically and as medicine)
insinuate in your ear, 'Mister, looking for
someone? I can get you a fifteen-year-old for
fifteen rupees, yes?'

I run the gauntlet of beggars, pimps and
pansies and turn into a four-foot-wide gulley.
I bang the latch of a door bearing a nameplate
in English and Urdu: '*Lutfunnissa Begam Dai*,
Midwife and Nurse.'

A girl's voice on the other side demands,
'Who is it?' She opens the door and slams it
in my face. '*Amma* (mother) is saying her
prayers . . . it's a Sikh,' she warns her mother.

I wait five minutes before I am let into
the little courtyard. It has nothing save a row
of earthen pitchers on one side, a gunny-sack
curtain to mark the latrine on the other, and
a charpoy or cot in the centre on which the
midwife is seated. She recognizes me. She

delivered my cook's wife of a son three months
ago and I paid her ten rupees for the service.

'*Salam valaikum*, Sardarji. How's the little
one?' she asks.

'He is well. And how is it with you and
your daughter?'

'Allah be thanked,' she says and raises
both her hands to the heavens. '*Beti* (daughter),
get some betel leaf for the Sardarji.' The
daughter goes indoors and re-emerges looking
like a miniature mobile tent, with holes in
front of her eyes.

Lutfunnissa is not poor by Indian
standards. She earns almost Rs 120 a month.
She has been twice divorced: by the first
husband because after many miscarriages she
produced only a daughter, and by the second
because she produced no children and he
married another woman who did. For some
years she lived in the same menage with her
co-wife. Then the younger woman persuaded
the husband to throw Lutfunnissa out.

All he had to do was to say 'I divorce
you,' three times and the break was
irrevocable. 'The holy Prophet—peace be
upon him—gave men the right to have four
wives at a time and discard those they did not

want,' she says. 'Who am I to question or
complain? Besides, I got my dowry from both
my husbands—Rs 750—and with it bought
this roof to cover my head,' she adds with a
weary smile, baring her betel-stained teeth.
'Now my only worry is my daughter. You
know she is almost thirteen! Once I find her
a husband, I can die peacefully.'

'You have many happy years before you.
You aren't too old to find another husband for
yourself.'

'*Toba, toba!* Heaven forbid!' she replies.
'You are teasing me. Who will marry an old
hag like me? Look at my white hair!' She
pulls a few strands across her eyes and is
pleased to see that none have turned white.

'Why haven't you sent your daughter to
school?'

'What will she do with education? Was I
educated? Did my mother or grandmother go
to school? Education puts wrong notions in
girls' heads. They want to go to the pictures;
they become fashionable and want to wear
rouge and lipstick; they want to do *gitpit*
(speak English) with strange men. No, Sardarji,
we are contented with our lot. She can cook
and sew. She can say her prayers from the

holy Koran. What more does anyone need?'

'How did you get to become a nurse?'

'Oh, that! My aunt was a midwife and I often went with her. Then I had to do a few weeks at the hospital to learn these new things about using antiseptic and keeping your hands clean. I haven't had many accidents. People come for me at all hours. Some pay Rs 7.50, some have nothing except a betel leaf. But Allah gives me enough to fill my belly.'

That ends the argument about education. Jahanara, the daughter, comes in accompanied by a woman in a burkha. Addressing the midwife, the visitor says, '*Amma* is in labour. Bring your things along.'

Lutfunnissa fetches her kit. It's all in an Air India sling bag, decorated with the mustachioed Maharajah bowing obsequiously. She dons her burkha and beckons me to go ahead. We come out into the lane. She chains the door of the house and puts a big iron lock in the ring. '*Beti*, bolt it from the inside.' I hear the bolt turn on the other side. 'Sardarji, these are bad times we live in. You cannot trust anyone; neither strangers nor your own kith and kin.'

Thirteen-year-old Jahanara locked from within and without, is symbolic of the state of emancipation Muslim women have achieved. It will be quite some time before their world changes.

Among Hindus, the pattern of relationship between men and women varies enormously in different regions and social classes. In the north, dominated by Muslims for many centuries, Hindu women draw a dupatta (head scarf) across their faces if they meet any of their husband's older male relatives. A wife will walk a few yards behind her husband, never alongside him. She will not sit on the same charpoy but on the floor; she will not eat with her husband, but only after he has finished eating.

Some Hindu communities preserve strange customs. The men among the Bishnois, a small group inhabiting a desert tract west of Delhi, choose the fittest young man in the community and make him *Gama shah ka saand*—the stud bull of Gama Shah, their legendary hero. The stud bull's main function is to impregnate wives of impotent or sterile Bishnois. When the men are at work in the fields, the stud visits homes of the needy. His ornate pair of slippers left conspicuously on the threshold indicates that the housewife is busy.

The hill people of the north-west have their own mores. They do not look upon their daughters as burdens since they do not have to provide dowries as large as those of people in the plains. On the contrary, in many cases the intending husband has to pay a bride price to the parents of the girl. Bride price is common among the poorer and lower castes such as the Kabirpanthi untouchables.

I acquired a Kabirpanthi family along with a house my wife inherited fourteen years ago in the small town of Kasauli in the Himalayas. At that time, Chajju Ram, the caretaker of the house, and his wife Kamala were in their twenties and had only one child. But every spring when we went up to Kasauli we found Kamala pregnant. Chajju Ram shamefacedly admitted to me: 'It is bitterly cold in the winter and we have only one quilt to cover ourselves.'

I provided them with another quilt but it did not affect Kamala's pregnancies.

They now have seven children living— five girls and two boys. Even Kamala does not remember the miscarriages and the number of children who died at birth. When questioned by my wife, she only wrung her hands and explained: 'What else have I to give him? It is a wife's duty. If I said no he might go to some other woman.'

When the two elder girls were four and two years old, they were betrothed to two brothers. Chajju Ram got Rs 225 for each of his daughters and invested the money in buying a buffalo.

Among the Kabirpanthis of Himachal, and many other Hindu tribes, *muklawa*, the consummation of marriage, takes place after the bride and groom have attained puberty. But neither of Chajju Ram's daughters had their *muklawa* with the boys originally chosen for them; their husbands, it turned out, were dwarfs. The marriages were annulled by amicable agreement between the parents. Chajju Ram returned the bride price. (In the meantime, the buffalo had borne many more buffaloes and brought him upto Rs 150 a month in milk.)

Both girls were married off a second time; one to an older man who had returned his barren wife to her parents, and the other to a

young attendant employed in an office.
Nothing was ever put down in writing. No
ritual was performed either at the marriages
or at the divorces. All that was necessary was
to have the approval of the Kabirpanthi
panchayat (council) and feed the bridegroom's
relatives and friends.

Two years ago Chajju Ram developed a
rasping cough and had to be admitted to a
sanitorium. He responded to treatment and
will be discharged from the sanitorium very
soon. Now only one worry clouds Kamala's
mind. '*Bibiji* (mistress),' she confided to my
wife, 'I do not want any more children. I
won't be able to have them in another few
years. Then I won't mind what he does. Why
don't you tell the doctor to tell him that it is
bad for his health?'

*

'If you study history,' Indira Gandhi once
said, 'you will find that where women have
risen, that country attained a high position,
and wherever they remained dormant, that
country slipped back.'

Two days after Mrs Gandhi was elected
prime minister, I went to a group of villages

along the Jamuna between Delhi and Agra.

Most of the land belonged to Brahmin agriculturists but there was a fair sprinkling of other castes—Jats, Gujjars, Harijans, Muslims, Meos and Sikhs. I joined a mixed group waiting for the ferry.

The men and women sat apart. The younger Hindu women covered their faces with their head scarves; some of the Muslim women wore burkhas. After talking to the men about things in general, I asked one, a Meo named Barkat from a small village, whether he knew who had been elected prime minister of India.

'It's Nehruji's daughter,' he replied. 'I don't recall her name.'

'Indira Gandhi,' volunteered a chorus of voices.

'Oh, yes, Indira Gandhi,' agreed Barkat. 'I knew it was Panditji's *chhokri* (lass).'

'How do you feel about having a woman as prime minister?' I asked the question loud enough to be heard by everyone.

For some time no one answered. I repeated the question, this time turning my face towards the women. '*Bhainji* (sister),' I asked, facing the eldest, 'what is your opinion?'

'*O Ruldu ki Ma* (mother of Ruldu), why don't you say something? At home you never stop jabbering.' This was a Jat from Faridabad. His wife was quick to retort, '*Ruldu ka Bap* (father of Ruldu), you who are so clever, why don't you reply?'

The peasants laughed. Their women giggled.

'It's good propaganda,' said a Sikh. 'People will think we are advanced. No other country in the world has a woman prime minister. I am all for it.'

'What is your opinion?' I asked, turning again to Barkat. I encouraged him: 'Women often rule in the home.'

'That's different,' exclaimed Barkat. Other villagers agreed with him. 'That's not the same thing.'

'Why?'

'Well, it's like this,' continued Barkat haltingly, 'If my wife makes a mistake, I slap her across the face. Who can slap the face of a prime minister?'

They sat pondering over the problem like philosophers. They drew patterns in the sand with their fingers. They looked for the boat that was to take them across the Jamuna.

Finally, the eldest spoke: 'The big question is, can a woman rule this country?' Then they drew more lines in the sand and again looked for the ferry.

This essay was written shortly after Indira Gandhi was elected prime minister.

Mother Teresa

It must have been more than twenty years ago that I was asked by the *New York Times* to do a profile of Mother Teresa for its magazine section. I wrote to Mother Teresa seeking her permission to call on her. And having got it, spent three days with her from the early hours of the morning to late at night. Nothing in my long journalistic career has remained as sharply etched in my memory as those three days with her in Calcutta. In my little study in my villa at Kasauli, I have only two pictures of the people I admire most—Mahatma Gandhi and Mother Teresa.

Before I met her face to face, I read Malcolm Muggeridge's book on Mother Teresa, *Something Beautiful for God*. Malcolm was a recent convert to Catholicism and prone to believe in miracles. He had gone to make a film on her for the British Broadcasting Corporation (BBC). They first went to the Nirmal Hriday (Sacred Heart) Home for dying destitutes close to the Kalighat temple. The team took some shots of the building from outside and of its sunlit courtyard. The camera crew was of the opinion that the interior was too dark and they had no artificial lights. However, since some footage was left, they decided to use it for interior shots. When the film was developed, the shots of the dormitories were found to be clearer than those taken in sunlight. The first thing I asked Mother Teresa was if this was true. She replied, 'But of course. Such things happen all the time.' And she added with increasing intensity of voice, 'Every day, every hour, every single minute, God manifests Himself in some miracle.'

She narrated other miracles of the days when her organization was little known and chronically short of cash. 'Money has never been much of a problem,' she told me. 'God gives through His people.' She told me that when she started her first school in the slums, she had no more than five rupees with her. But as soon as people came to know what she was doing, they brought money and other things. 'It was all divine providence.' One winter they ran out of quilts. Her nuns found sheets but there was no money to buy cotton. Just as Mother Teresa was about to rip open her own pillow, the bell rang. Some official

who was about to leave Calcutta for a posting
abroad had brought his quilts and mattresses
to give them away. On another occasion when
they had run out of rations, a lady they had
never seen before left them a bag of rice. 'We
measured the rice with our little tin cup; it
was exactly what we required for the day.
When I told the lady that, she broke down
and cried as she realized that God had used
her as an instrument of His will.'

The first institution she took me to was
Nirmal Hriday. It was in 1952 that the Calcutta
Corporation had handed the building to her.
Orthodox Hindus were outraged. Four
hundred Brahmin priests attached to the Kali
temple demonstrated outside the building.
'One day I went out and spoke to them. "If
you want to kill me, kill me. But do not
disturb the inmates. Let them die in peace." '
That silenced them. Then one of the priests
staggered in. He was in an advanced stage of
galloping phthisis. The nuns looked after him
till he died. That changed the priests' attitude
towards Mother Teresa. Later one day,
another priest entered the Home, prostrated
himself at Mother Teresa's feet and said, 'For
thirty years I have served the Goddess Kali in

her temple. Now the Goddess stands before me.'

I went around Nirmal Hriday with Mother Teresa. In the hour we were there, of the 170 men and women lying in rows, two died. Their beds were quickly taken by two lying on the floor of the veranda outside. Mother Teresa went round to every one of the inmates and asked them how they were. Her only message of cheer to people who knew they had not much longer to live was '*Bhogoban acchen*'—there is God.

Mother Teresa did not make an impressive figure—barely five feet tall and very slim, high cheek bones and thin lips. And a face full of wrinkles. It was a homely face without any charisma. Muggeridge was right in describing her as a unique person, 'but not in the vulgar celebrity sense of having neon lighting about her head. Rather in the opposite sense—of someone who has merged herself in the common face of mankind.' The nun's dress she had designed for herself would make the plainest-looking woman look plainer.

She spoke with an Indian lilt in her voice. And like most convent-bred Indians, ended her sentences with an interrogatory 'No?',

meaning 'isn't that so?' She told me how at
the age of twelve she had dared to become a
nun and left her parental home in Skopje
(Yugoslavia); how she had learnt English in a
Dublin convent and had come to Calcutta in
1929 as a geography teacher in St Mary's
High School. She was for many years, principal
of the school. Then suddenly a strange
restlessness came over her. It was, as she
describes it, 'a special call from Jesus Christ.'
10 September 1946 was her 'day of decision'
as well as 'inspiration day'. This is how she
put it: 'I was going to Darjeeling to make my
retreat. It was in that train that I heard the
call to give up all and follow Him to the slums
and serve Him among the poorest of the
poor.' She prepared herself for her mission,
receiving an intensive course in nursing at
Patna. In 1948 she opened her first school in
the slums of Calcutta in a private house
donated to her. Her only helper was Subhasini
Das (Sister Agnes). A new order, the
Missionaries of Charity, was instituted. A male
branch, Brothers of Charity, came up some
years later, and initiates had to take four
vows—poverty, chastity, obedience and
wholehearted service to the poor.

Mother Teresa taught herself Bengali which she was soon able to speak fluently. When India became independent, she took Indian nationality. Her strength came from simple convictions. ('She is blessed with certainties,' writes Muggeridge.) When I asked her, 'Who has been the dominant figure in your life—Gandhi, Nehru, Albert Schweitzer?', without a pause she replied, 'Jesus Christ'. When I followed it up with a question about books that might have impressed her, her answer was equally categorical and in the singular: 'The Bible'.

The day I accompanied Mother Teresa on a 'begging' expedition, we boarded a crowded tram car. A man immediately stood up to offer her his seat. Another untied a knot in his dhoti and took out change to buy her ticket. The ticket conductor refused to take money from her and punched a ticket for which he paid himself. We arrived at the office of a large biscuit factory. Mr Mukherjee, the manager, had his excuses ready. His business was not doing well, he was having union problems, and so on. Mother Teresa expressed sympathy with him. 'We only want the broken biscuits you discard. Thank God,

we have no union problems. We work for
God; there are no unions.' I could see Mr
Mukherjee's defences crumble. He picked
up his phone and ordered forty large tins of
broken biscuits to be delivered to Mother
Teresa.

Recognition came to Mother Teresa when
in 1962, she was awarded the Padma Shri.
Both Pandit Nehru and his sister Vijayalakshmi
Pandit who were present at the investiture,
admitted that they almost broke down with
emotion. A few months later came the
Magsaysay Award. Pope Paul VI presented
her with a car; she auctioned it and raised
four-and-a-half lakh rupees. In 1971 she was
awarded the Pope John XXIII prize of 21,500
US dollars. Then came the Good Samaritans
and the Joseph Kennedy awards and the
Templeton Foundation Prize. While making
the presentation, Prince Philip referred to the
'sheer goodness which shines through Mother
Teresa's life and work, and inspires humility,
wonder and admiration.'

Since then, till she got the Nobel Prize
for peace, there was not a month when she
was not showered with money and awards of
some kind or another. Every paise went in

the upkeep of hospitals, orphanages and leprosaria that she opened in different parts of India as well as in foreign countries.

One evening, returning from Sealdah to her home, we had to get out of our car as there was a mammoth funeral procession coming from the opposite direction. It was the cortège of Muzaffar Ahmed, one of the founding fathers of communism in India. As we proceeded on our way, men waving little red flags stepped out of their ranks to touch Mother Teresa's feet, receive her blessings, and then rejoin the procession.

Mother Teresa dropped me at Dum Dum airport. As I was about to take leave of her she said, 'So?', meaning whether I had anything else to ask. 'Tell me how you can touch people with loathsome diseases like leprosy and gangrene. Aren't you revolted by people filthy with dysentry and cholera vomit?'

She replied, 'I see Jesus in every human being. I say to myself: this is hungry Jesus, I must feed him. This is sick Jesus. This one has gangrene, dysentry and cholera. I must wash him and tend to him. I serve them because I love Jesus.'

The last time I saw Mother Teresa was

two years ago when she came to Delhi to receive two Maruti vans presented to her by my friend H.N. Sikand. There was an enormous crowd at his home. Mother Teresa passed by me without recognizing me. How could she, after all those years and the millions of people she must have met.

Sex in Indian Life

Many winters ago I happened to be travelling by a night train from Delhi to Bhopal. It was an express that made a few halts at major stations. I found myself in a compartment of five berths: three below and two on the sides above. I had a lower berth as did the other two passengers who were there before me. The upper berths were reserved in the names of Professor and Mrs Saxena. Fifteen minutes before the train was due to leave, a party of men and women escorting a bride decked in an ornate sari drawn discreetly across her face and her arm loaded with ivory bangles stopped by our compartment, read the names on the panel and came in. They were dismayed to see the two berths reserved for them separated by a fifteen-foot chasm of space. One of the party approached me and asked if I could take one of the upper berths to accommodate the newly-weds. I readily agreed and moved my bedding roll. Another passenger who had the middle berth also moved up on the other upper berth so that the bridal couple could be alongside each other. I heard one of the party

stop the conductor and tell him to wake up
the couple at a particular junction where the
train was to make a brief three-minute halt at
3 a.m.

As the conductor blew his whistle and
waved his green flag, the party took leave of
the bridal couple with much embracing and
sobbing. No sooner had the train cleared the
lighted platform than the bride blew her nose
and uncovered her face. She was in her mid-
twenties: pale-skinned, round-faced and
wearing thick glasses. I couldn't see much of
her figure but my guess was that she would
be forever fighting a losing battle against fat.
Her groom looked a couple of years older
than her (the 'professor' being honorific for a
junior lecturer) and like his bride, was sallow-
faced, corpulent and bespectacled. From the
snatches of conversation that I could hear (I
was only four feet above them), I gathered
that they were total strangers and their
marriage had been arranged by relatives and
through the matrimonial columns of *The
Hindustan Times*. They talked of their papajis
and mummyjis. Then of their time in college
(the halcyon days for most educated Indians)
and of their friends: 'like a brother to me' or

'better than my own real sister'. After a while
the conversation began to flag; I saw the
man's hand resting on his woman's, on the
window sill.

The lights were switched off leaving only
a nightlight which bathed the compartment
in a moonlight blue. I could not see very
much except when the train ran past brightly-
lit platforms of wayside railway stations.

The couple did not bother to use the
middle berth vacated for them and decided to
make themselves as comfortable as they could
on a four-foot wide wooden plank. They
ignored the presence of the other passengers
in the small compartment and were totally
absorbed in getting to know each other. Such
was their impatience that they did not find
the time to change into more comfortable
clothes. They drew a quilt over themselves
and were lost to the world.

The sari is a costume that is both very
ornamental as well as functional. Properly
draped, it can accentuate the contours of the
female form giving a special roundness to the
buttocks. A well-cut blouse worn with the sari
elevates the bosom and exposes the belly to
below the navel. There is no other form of

female attire which can both conceal physical shortcomings of the wearer as well as expose what deserves exposure. A fat woman looks less fat in a sari than she would in a dress, and a thin woman looks more filled in. At the same time, a sari is very functional. All a woman has to do when she wants to urinate or defecate is to lift it to her waist. When required to engage in a quick sexual intercourse, she needs to do no more than draw it up a little and open up her thighs. Apparently this was what Mrs Saxena was called upon to do. I heard a muffled cry of 'Hai Ram' escape her lips and realized that the marriage had been consummated.

The Saxenas did not get up to go to the bathroom to wash themselves but began a repeat performance. This time they were less impatient and seemed to be getting more out of their efforts. More than once the quilt slipped off them and I caught a glimpse of the professor's heaving buttocks and his bride's bosoms which he had extricated out of her choli. Above the rattle and whish of the speeding train I heard the girl's whimper and the man's exulting grunts. They had a third go at each other before peace descended on our compartment. It was then well past midnight. Thereafter it was only the wail of the engine tearing through the dark night and the snores of my elderly companions that occasionally disturbed my slumber.

We were rudely woken by someone thumping on the door, slapping the window panes and yelling, 'Get up! get up! It is Sehore. The train will leave in another minute.' It was the conductor.

I turned the switch on and the compartment was flooded with light. A memorable sight it was! Professor Saxena fast asleep with his buttocks exposed; Mrs Saxena also fast asleep, her mouth wide open, breasts bare, lying supine like a butterfly pinned on a board. Her hair was scattered on her pillow. Their glasses lay on the floor.

Whatever embarrassment they felt was drowned in the hustle and bustle of getting off the train. We heaved out their beds and suitcases. The professor stumbled out onto the cold platform adjusting his flies. His wife followed him covering her bare bosom with a flap of her sari. As the train began to move, she screamed—one of her earrings was missing. The friendly guard brought the train

to a halt. All of us went down on our knees
scouring the floor. The errant earring was
found wedged in a crevice of the seat. We
resumed our journey.

'It is love,' remarked one of my travelling
companions ,with great understanding. 'They
are newly married and this was their first
night together. All should be forgiven for
people in love.'

'What kind of love?' I asked in a sarcastic
tone.

'A few hours ago they were complete
strangers. They haven't the patience to wait
till they get home; they start having sex
without as much as exchanging a word of
affection. You call that love?'

'Well,' he replied pondering over the
episode. 'They may not get another chance
for some days. There will be his relatives, his
mother, sisters, brothers. And lots of religious
ceremonies. Youth is impatient and the body
has its own compulsions. Let us say it is the
beginning of love.'

'It may be the beginning of another
family, but I don't see where love comes in,'
I remarked. 'I can understand illiterate
peasants coupling like the cattle they rear,

but I cannot understand two educated people—a lecturer in a college and a school teacher—lacking so totally in sophistication or sense of privacy as to begin copulating in the presence of three strangers.'

'You have foreign ideas,' said the third man dismissing me. 'Anyway, it is 3.30 in the morning. Let's get some sleep.' He switched off the light and the argument.

The episode stayed in my mind because it vividly illustrated the pattern of the man-woman relationship that obtains among the vast majority of Indians. Love as the word is understood in the west is known only to a tiny minority of the very westernized living in the half-a-dozen big cities of India, who prefer to speak English rather than Indian languages, read only English books, watch only Western movies and even dream in English. For the rest, it is something they read about in poems or see on the screen but very rarely experience personally. Arranged marriages are the accepted norm; 'love' marriages, a rarity. In arranged marriages, the parties first make each other's acquaintance physically through the naked exploration of each other's bodies, and it is only after some

of the lust has been drained out of their
systems that they get the chance to discover
each other's minds and personalities. It is
only after lust begins to lose its potency and
there is no clash of temperaments that the
alliance may, in later years, develop bonds of
companionship. But the chances of this
happening are bleak. In most cases, they
suffer each other till the end of their days.

I have no idea what became of the
Saxenas whose nuptial consummation I had
been witness to. It is likely that by now they
had produced a small brood of Saxenas. He is
probably a full professor teaching romantic
poetry and occasionally penning a verse or
two to some younger lady professor ('like a
sister to me') or to some pig-tailed student
('like my own daughter'). Mrs Saxena probably
tries to retain her husband's interest through
dog-like devotion and prayer and with the
help of charms brought from 'holy' men. On
the rare occasions when the professor mounts
her, she has to fantasize about one of his
younger colleagues ('exactly like a real brother
to me') before she shudders in the throes of
an orgasm with the name of God on her
lips—'*Hai Ram*'.

The Saxenas are luckier than most Indian couples because they live away from their families and are assured a certain amount of privacy. To most newly-married Indian couples, the concept of privacy is as alien as that of love. They rarely get a room to themselves; the bride-wife sleeps with women members of her husband's family; the husband shares his charpoy placed alongside his father's and brothers'. Occasionally the mother-in-law, anxious to acquire a grandson, will contrive a meeting between her son and his wife: the most common technique is to get her to take a tumbler of milk to the lad when other male members are elsewhere. The lad grabs the chance for the 'quickie'. Hardly ever does the couple get enough time for a prolonged and satisfying bout of intercourse. Most Indian men are not even aware that women also have orgasms; most Indian women share this ignorance because although they go from one pregnancy to another, they have no idea that sex can be pleasurable. This is a sad commentary on the people of the country that produced the most widely-read treatise on the art of sex, the *Kama Sutra*, and elevated the act of sex to spiritual sublimity by explicit depictions on its temples.

Phoolan Devi

It was the afternoon of Saturday, 14 February 1981. Winter had given way to spring. Amidst the undulating sea of ripening wheat and green lentil were patches of bright yellow mustard in flower. Skylarks rose from the ground, suspended themselves in the blue skies and poured down song on the earth below. Allah was in His heaven and all was peace and tranquillity in Behmai.

Behmai is a tiny hamlet along the river Jamuna inhabited by about fifty families belonging mainly to the Thakur caste, with a sprinkling of shepherds and ironsmiths. Although it is only eighty miles from the industrial metropolis, Kanpur, it has no road connecting it to any town. To get to Behmai you have to traverse dusty footpaths meandering through cultivated fields, and go down narrow, snake-infested ravines choked with camelthorn and elephant grass. It is not surprising that till the middle of February, few people had heard of Behmai. After what happened on Saturday the 14th, it was on everyone's lips.

There was not much to do in the fields except drive off wild pigs and deer. Some boys armed with catapults and loud voices were out doing this; others played on the sand bank while their buffaloes wallowed in the mud. Men dozed on their charpoys; women sat in huddles gossiping as they ground corn or picked lice out of their children's hair.

No one in Behmai noticed a party dressed in police uniforms cross the river. It was led by a young woman with cropped hair wearing the khaki coat of a deputy superintendent of police with three silver stars, blue jeans and boots with zippers. She wore lipstick and her nails had varnish on them. Her belt was charged with bullets and had a curved Gurkha knife—a *kokri*—attached to it. A Sten gun was slung across her shoulders and she carried a battery-fitted megaphone in her hand. The party sat down beside the village shrine adorned with the trident emblem of Shiva, the God of destruction.

The eldest of the party, a notorious gangster named Baba Mustaqeem, instructed the group on how to go about their job: A dozen men were to surround the village so that no one could get out; the remaining men,

led by the woman, were to search all the
houses and take whatever they liked. But no
women were to be raped nor anyone except
the two men they were looking for, to be
slain. They listened in silence and nodded
their heads in agreement. They touched the
base of Shiva's trident for good luck and
dispersed.

The girl in the officer's uniform went up
on the parapet of the village well, switched
on the megaphone and shouted at the top of
her voice, 'Listen you fellows! You *bhosreekey*
(progenies of the cunt)! If you love your lives,
hand over all the cash, silver and gold you
have. And listen again! I know those
madarchods (motherfuckers) Lal Ram Singh
and Shri Ram Singh are hiding in this village.
If you don't hand them over to me I will stick
my gun into your bums and tear them apart.
You've heard me. This is Phoolan Devi
speaking. If you don't get cracking, you know
what Phoolan Devi will do to you. *Jai* Durga
Mata (Victory to the Mother Goddess, Durga)!'
She raised her gun and fired a single shot in
the air to convince them that she meant what
she said.

Phoolan Devi stayed at the well while

her men went looting the Thakurs' homes.
Women were stripped of their earrings, nose
pins, silver bangles and anklets. Men handed
over whatever cash they had on their persons.
The operation lasted almost an hour. But
there was no trace of Lal Ram Singh or Shri
Ram Singh. The people of the village denied
ever having seen them. 'You are lying!' roared
Phoolan Devi. 'I will teach you to tell the
truth.' She ordered all the young men to be
brought before her. About thirty were dragged
out to face her. She asked them again, 'You
motherfuckers, unless you tell me where those
two sons of pigs are, I will roast you alive.'
The men pleaded with her and swore they
had never seen the two men.

'Take these fellows along,' she ordered
her men. 'I'll teach them a lesson they will
never forget.' The gang pushed the thirty
villagers out of Behmai along the path leading
to the river. At an embankment, she ordered
them to be halted and lined up. 'For the last
time, will you tell me where those two bastards
are, or do I have to kill you?' she asked
pointing her Sten gun at them. The villagers
again pleaded ignorance. 'If we knew, we
would tell you.' 'Turn round,' thundered

Phoolan Devi. 'The men turned their faces towards the green embankment. '*Bhosreekey*, this will also teach you not to report to the police. Shoot the bloody bastards!' she ordered her men and yelled, '*Jai* Durga *Mata*!' There was a burst of gunfire. The thirty men crumpled to the earth. Twenty died; the others hit in their limbs or buttocks lay sprawled in blood-spattered dust.

Phoolan Devi and her murderous gang went down the path yelling, '*Jai* Durga *Mata*! *Jai* Baba Mustaqeem! *Jai* Bikram Singh! *Jai* Phoolan Devi!'

The next morning, the massacre of Behmai made front-page headlines in all newspapers all over India.

*

Dacoity in India is as old as history. In some regions it is endemic and no sooner are some gangs liquidated than others come up. The most notorious dacoit country is a couple of hundred miles south-west of Behmai, along the ravines of the Chambal river in Madhya Pradesh. In the Bundelkhand district of Uttar Pradesh in which Behmai is located, it is of comparatively recent origin and the State police suspect that when things became too hot around the Chambal, some gangs migrated to Bundelkhand where the terrain was very much like the one they were familiar with. The river Jamuna, after its descent from the Himalayas, runs a sluggish, serpentine course past Delhi and Agra into Bundelkhand. Here it passes through a range of low-lying hills covered with dense forests. Several monsoon-fed rivulets running through deep gorges join it as it goes on to meet the holy Ganga at Allahabad. It is wild and beautiful country: hills, ravines and forests enclosing small picturesque hamlets. By day there are peacocks and multicoloured butterflies; by night, nightjars calling to each other across the pitch-black wilderness flecked by fireflies. Nilgai, spotted deer, wild boar, hyena, jackal and fox abound. It is also infested with snakes, the commonest being cobras, the most venomous of the species. Cultivation is sparse and entirely dependent on rain. The chief produce are lentils and wheat. The peasantry is amongst the poorest in the country. The two main communities living along the river banks are Mallahs (boatmen) and Thakurs. The Thakurs are the higher caste and own

most of the land. The Mallahs are amongst
the lowest in the Hindu caste hierarchy, own
little land and live mostly by plying boats,
fishing and distilling liquor. Till recently,
dacoit gangs were mixed: Thakurs, Mallahs,
Yadavs (cattlemen), Gujjars (milkmen) and
Muslims. But now, more and more are tending
to becoming caste-oriented. There is little
love lost between the Thakurs and the
Mallahs. Behmai is a Thakur village; Phoolan
Devi, a Mallahin.

No stigma is attached to being a dacoit;
in their own territory they are known as *bagis*
or rebels. Hindi movies, notably the box office
hit of all time, *Sholay*, in which the hero is a
dacoit, has added romance to the profession
of banditry.

Dacoit gangs are well-equipped with
automatic weapons, including self-loading
rifles acquired mostly through raids. A police
note on anti-dacoity operations records that
Jalaun district which includes Behmai, has
fifteen gangs of between ten to thirty members
each operating in the area. Phoolan Devi and
her current paramour, Man Singh Yadav, have
fifteen men with them. In the last six months,
the police have had ninety-three encounters

with dacoits in which they killed 159 and captured 137. Forty-seven surrendered themselves. 439 still roam about the jungles and ravines, hunting and being hunted.

I sat on the parapet of the village well, on the same spot from where Phoolan Devi had announced her arrival in Behmai a year and a half earlier. In front of me sat village men, women and children and the police escort provided for me. An old woman wailed, 'That Mallahin killed my husband and two sons. May she die a dog's death!' A man stood up and bared his belly which showed gun-shot scars. Another bared his buttocks and pointed to a dimple where a bullet had hit him.

'Can any of you tell me why Phoolan Devi came to this village and killed so many people?' I asked.

No one answered.

'Is it true that Lal Ram Singh and Shri Ram Singh were in Behmai?'

A chorus of voices answered: 'No, we have never seen them.'

'Is it true that a few months before the dacoity they had brought Phoolan Devi with them, raped her for several weeks before she managed to escape?'

'*Ram! Ram!*' protested some of them. 'We had never seen the Mallahin in this village before the dacoity.'

'Why then, did she ask for the two brothers? How did she know her way about this village?'

No one answered.

'You will not get anything out of these fellows,' the police inspector said to me in English. 'You know what these villagers are! They never tell the truth.'

I gave up my cross-examination and decided to go around Behmai. I started from the village shrine with the Shiva's trident, came back to the well and then to the embankment where she had killed the twenty men. I went up a mound where the police had set up a sentry box from which I could get a bird's-eye view of the village, the Jamuna and the country beyond. The police sentinel on duty who had been in the village for several weeks volunteered the following information: 'Sir, I think I can tell you why Phoolan Devi did what she did. You see that village across the Jamuna on top of the hill? It is called Pal, it is a Mallah village. Mallahs used to come through Behmai to take the ferry. Thakur boys used to tease their girls and beat up their men. I am told there were several instances when they stripped the girls naked and forced them to dance. The Mallahs appealed to Phoolan Devi to teach these Thakurs a lesson. She had her own reasons as well. Her lover Bikram Singh had been murdered by Thakurs Lal Ram Singh and his twin brother Shri Ram Singh. And they had kept her imprisoned in this village for several weeks raping and beating her. She managed to escape and rejoin her gang. She also suspected that these fellows have been informing the police of her movements. It was revenge, pure and simple.'

*

'For every man this girl has killed, she has slept with two,' said the superintendent of police in charge of 'Operation Phoolan Devi'. The police estimate the number of men slain by her or one of her gang in the last year and a half to be over thirty. There is no way of finding out the exact number of men she murdered or was laid by. But it is certain that not all the killings nor the copulations were entirely of her own choosing. On many occasions she happened to be with bandits who were trigger-happy; and being the only woman in a gang of a dozen or more, she was regarded by them as their common property. She accepted the rules of the game and had to give herself to them in turn. It was more a resignation to being raped than the craving for sex of a nymphomaniac.

I was able to reconstruct Phoolan Devi's past by talking to her parents, sisters and one of her lovers, and cross-checking what they told me with a statement she made to the police on 6 January 1979, the first time she was arrested. This was in connection with a robbery in the house of her cousin with whom her father had had a dispute over land. Some stolen goods were recovered from her. She spent a fortnight in police custody. Her statement is prefaced by a noting made by the officer. He describes her as 'about twenty years old; wheatish complexion, oval face; short but sturdily built.' Phoolan Devi stated: 'I am the second daughter of a family of six consisting of five girls. The youngest is a boy, Shiv Narain Singh. We belong to the Mallah caste and live in the village Gurh-Ka-Purwa. At the age of twelve I was given away in marriage to a forty-five-year-old widower, Putti Lal.' Then she talks of her second 'marriage' to Kailash in Kanpur. The rest of her life story was narrated to me by her mother, Muli. 'Phoolan Devi was too young to consummate her marriage and came back to us after a few days. A year or two later, we sent her back to her husband. This time she stayed with him for a few months but was unhappy. She came away without her husband's permission, determined not to go back to him.' It would appear that she had been deflowered. Her mother describes her as being 'filled up'—an Indian expression for a girl whose bosom and behind indicate that she has had sex. It would appear that she had developed an appetite for sex which her ageing husband could not fulfil. Her parents were distraught: a girl leaving her husband brought disgrace to the family. 'I told her to drop dead,' said her mother. 'I told her to jump in a well or drown herself in the Jamuna; we would not have a married daughter living with us. Putti Lal came and took away the silver ornaments he had given her and married another woman. What were we to do? We started looking for another husband for her, but it is not easy to find a husband for a

discarded girl, is it?' she asked me. Phoolan
Devi kept out of her parents' way as much as
she could by taking the family's buffaloes out
for grazing. She began to liaise with the son
of the village headman. (In rural India such
affairs are consummated in lentil or sugarcane
fields.) The headman's son invited his friends
to partake of the feast. Phoolan Devi had no
choice but to give in. The village gossip mill
ground out stories of Phoolan Devi being
available to anyone who wanted to lay her.
Her mother admitted, 'The family's *pojeeshun*
(position) was compromised; our noses were
cut. We decided to send her away to her
sister, Ramkali, who lives in Teonga village
across the river.'

It did not take long for Phoolan Devi to
find another lover in Teonga. This was a
distant cousin, Kailash, married and with four
children. Kailash had contacts with a dacoit
gang. He gives a vivid account of how he was
seduced by Phoolan Devi. 'One day I was
washing my clothes on the banks of the
Jamuna. This girl brought her sister's buffaloes
to wallow in the shallows of the river. We got
talking. She asked me to lend her my cake of
soap so that she could bathe herself. I gave

her what remained of the soap. She stripped herself before my eyes. While she splashed water on herself and soaped her bosom and buttocks, she kept talking to me. I got very excited watching her. After she was dressed, I followed her into the lentil fields. I threw her on the ground and mounted her. I was too worked up and was finished in no time. I begged her to meet me again. She agreed to come the next day at the same time and at the same place.

'We made love many times. But it was never enough. She started playing hard to get. 'If you want me, you must marry me. Then I'll give you all you want,' she said. I told her I had a wife and children and could only have her as my mistress. She would not let me touch her unless I agreed to marry her. I became desperate. I took her with me to Kanpur. A lawyer took fifty rupees from me, wrote something on a piece of paper and told us that we were man and wife. We spent two days in Kanpur. During the day we went to the movies; at night we made love and slept in each other's arms. When we returned to Teonga, my parents refused to take us in. We spent a night out in the fields. The next day

I told Phoolan Devi to go back to her parents
as I had decided to return to my wife and
children. She swore she would kill me. I have
not seen her since. But I am afraid one of
these days she will get me.'

'What does your Phoolania look like?' I
asked Kailash. 'I am told her sister Ramkali
resembles her.'

'Phoolan is slightly shorter, lighter-skinned
and has a nicer figure. She is much better-
looking than Ramkali.'

'I am told she uses very bad language.'

'She never spoke harshly to me; to me
she spoke only the language of love.'

Phoolan Devi had more coming to her. A
few days after she had been turned out by
Kailash, she ran into Kailash's wife Shanti, at
a village fair. Shanti pounced on Phoolan, tore
her hair, clawed her face and in front of the
crowd that had collected, abused her: 'Whore!
Bitch! Homebreaker!' What was known only
to a few hamlets now became common
knowledge: Phoolan was a slut. As if this were
not enough, the village headman's son who
was under the impression that Phoolan was
exclusively at his beck and call, heard of her
escapade with Kailash. He summoned her to

his house and thrashed her with his shoes. Thus, at the age of eighteen, Phoolan found herself discarded by everyone. Her parents did not want her, her old husband had divorced her, her second 'marriage' had come to naught, she had been laid by men none of whom was willing to take her as a wife. It seemed to her that no one in the world wanted to have anything to do with her. She had only two choices before her: to go to some distant city and become a prostitute, or kill herself. There were times she considered throwing herself into the well.

Unknown to her, there was someone who had taken a fancy to her. This was young Bikram Singh, a friend of Kailash and member of a gang of dacoits led by a man called Babu Gujjar. Bikram Singh had seen Phoolan around the village and heard stories of her performances in the lentil fields. One afternoon he came to Gurh-Ka-Purwa with some of his gang and bluntly told Phoolan's parents that he had come to take away their daughter. Phoolan was adamant. 'I will talk to you with my sandals,' she said spitting on the ground. Bikram hit her with a whip he was carrying. Phoolan Devi fled from the village

and went to stay with her other sister,
Rukmini, in the village Orai. It was there that
she heard that a warrant for arrest had been
issued against her and Kailash for the dacoity
in her cousin's house. The man who took her
to the police station raped her before handing
her over. She spent a fortnight in jail. When
she returned home, Bikram came to see her
again. He threatened her: 'Either you come
with me or I take your brother Shiv Narain
with me.' Phoolan was very attached to her
only brother; he was eleven years old and
studying in the village school. After some
wrangling, she agreed to go with Bikram.

Kailash describes Bikram Singh as fair,
tall and wiry. Bikram was obviously very taken
with Phoolan. He had her long hair cropped.
He gave her a transistor radio and cassette
recorder as she was inordinately fond of
listening to film music. He bought her a
khaki shirt and jeans. He taught her how to
handle a gun. She proved a very adept disciple
and was soon a crack shot.

For the first time in her life Phoolan felt
wanted by someone. She responded to
Bikram's affection and began to describe
herself as his beloved. She had a rubber

stamp made for herself which she used as a letterhead in the letters she got written on her behalf. It reads: '*Dasyu Sundari, Dasyu Samrat* Bikram Singh *ki Premika*' (Dacoit Beauty, Beloved of Bikram Singh King of Dacoits).

Being the 'beloved of Bikram' did not confer any special privileges on Phoolan. Whether she liked it or not, she had to serve the rest of the gang. At the time, the leader happened to be Babu Gujjar, a singularly rough customer. He had his own way of expressing his superiority over his gang. He liked to have sex in broad daylight and in front of the others. So Phoolan Devi had to submit to being ravished and brutalized by Babu Gujjar in public. When her turn came to be made love to by Bikram, she complained to him about the indignity. By then, Bikram had developed a strong sense of possession over Phoolan. He did not have the courage to admit it, but one night while Babu Gujjar was asleep, he shot him in the head. Bikram Singh became the leader of the gang and at Phoolan's insistence, forbade the others from touching her. There wasn't much resentment because the gang soon acquired another

woman, Kusum Nain, who happened to be
better-looking than Phoolan. Kusum, a
Thakur, attached herself to the Thakur
brothers, Lal Ram Singh and Shri Ram Singh.
The two women became jealous of each other.

Despite her many unpleasant experiences
with men, Phoolan Devi did not give up her
habit of cock-teasing. She sensed that her full
bosom and rounded buttocks set men's minds
aflame with lust. Nevertheless, she persisted
in bathing in the presence of the men of her
gang. One gangster, now in police custody,
who had known her as well as Kusum Nain
and Meera Thakur (other female dacoits, since
then slain) vouches for this: 'The other girls
were as tough as Phoolan but they observed
certain proprieties in the company of men.
They would go behind a tree or bushes to
take a bath. Not Phoolan; she took off her
clothes in front of us as if we did not exist.
The other girls used language becoming to
women. Phoolan is the most foul-mouthed
wench I have ever met. Every time she opens
her mouth she uses the foulest of abuse—
bhosreekey, *gaandu* (bugger), *madarchod*, *betichod*
(daughterfucker).'

The inspector of police has in his files a

sheaf of letters written to him on behalf of
Phoolan Devi. They are a delightful mixture
of the sacred and the profane, of high falutin
Hindi and sheer obscenity. The one he read
out to me began with salutations to the Mother
Goddess under her printed letterhead. The
text ran somewhat as follows:

Honourable and Respected Inspector General
Sahib,

I learn from several Hindi journals that you
have been making speeches saying that you
will have us dacoits shot like pie-dogs. I
hereby give you notice that if you do not stop
bakwas (nonsense) of this kind, I will have
your revered mother abducted and so
thoroughly fucked by my men that she will
need medical attention. So take heed.

It is more than likely that Bikram Singh,
besides keeping Phoolan Devi exclusively for
himself, also claimed his right as the leader,
to enjoy the company of Kusum Nain as well.
This irked the Thakur brothers. They left
Bikram's gang and looked out for an
opportunity to kill him. On the night of
13 August 1980, they trapped and slew Bikram
Singh. It is believed that the murder was

committed in Behmai, and that the Thakurs
unceremoniously kicked Bikram's corpse
before it was thrown into the river.

Lal Ram Singh and Shri Ram Singh
retained Phoolan Devi in Behmai. They
brutalized and humiliated her in front of the
entire village. One night, on the pretext of
wanting to relieve herself, Phoolan Devi
managed to vanish into the darkness. She
crossed the Jamuna over to the Mallah village,
Pal. From there she got in touch with the
Muslim gangster Baba Mustaqeem and
pleaded with him to help her avenge the
murder of Bikram Singh. Mustaqeem agreed.
This is how she ended up being at Behmai on
the afternoon of 14 February 1981.

Ghayoorunnisa Hafeez

Ghayoorunnisa Hafeez of Hyderabad came
into my life when I was seventeen years old.
She was a couple of years older and had come
to Delhi to join Lady Hardinge Medical
College where her elder sister was studying.

After a year of medical studies she joined
Lady Irwin College to take a degree in home
science. My younger sister was a student
there. The two girls became friends. She was
invited to our home for a weekend.

She came draped in a burkha. At my
sister's insistence she took it off and was
introduced to the family. For me it was a
bewitching experience. The art of unveiling
is a dramatic event, as spectacular as when a
curtain goes up in a theatre revealing a stage
brightly lit with coloured lights, resembling a
fairyland.

My first impression was that she was
beautiful beyond compare. She was a small,
frail girl with a sallow complexion and curly
light brown hair. She spoke English without
any regional accent. Her Urdu was delightfully
Dakhhani. What really bowled me over was

that a girl who had spent so many of her adolescent years in seclusion could be so saucy and forward.

A few days after she came to our home for the first time, my sister and I took her to the pictures. I sat between the two girls. No sooner were the lights dimmed than she took my hand under the folds of her sari. I was wild with joy.

She once got permission to spend an evening at our home. I went to pick her up and instead of taking her home, I took her for a long drive around New Delhi. At that time it was still sparsely populated and the ridge was a welcome wilderness. We never got beyond holding hands and exchanging words of affection. She was very firm about how far unmarried people could go in getting to know each other.

We wrote long letters to each other. We continued writing to each other in the years I was in England. Her letters got shorter and rarer and then stopped altogether. I learnt from my sister that Ghayoor had got married to a Muslim army officer who also belonged to Hyderabad.

Why I regard my brief and near-platonic

relationship with Ghayoor an important landmark in my life is because it changed my attitude towards Muslims.

Like other Hindus and Sikhs of my generation, I had been brought up on anti-Muslim prejudices based on Muslim stereotypes.

The first awakening came with my close association with the saintly *maulvi* Shaifuddin Nayyar, my Urdu teacher. A more upright and God-fearing man I had not met in my childhood.

Then came Ghayoorunnisa Hafeez who proved to me that members of the two communities could love each other. Once you fall in love with someone of another community, you fall in love with all her people. And finally there was Manzur Qadir. After coming to know these people, I came to the naïve conclusion that an Indian Muslim could do no wrong.

Ghayoorunnisa resurfaced in my life thirty years later. My sister had asked me over for breakfast at my parents' home. When I arrived there she asked me, 'Do you recognize this girl?' Of course! It was Ghayoor. She was no longer a girl but a middle-aged woman who had buried two husbands. With her was a comely teenager, Fareesa, her daughter from her first husband. Fareesa joined Lady Irwin College. I was appointed her local guardian. Fareesa was very popular with college boys. Whenever she went out with them she left a note saying that she was going to see her local guardian. She had no problem extracting a letter from me stating that she had spent the evening in my home.

Fareesa spent her first honeymoon with her English husband at my house. She later divorced him and married a Swedish banker. They live in style in Hong Kong. Whenever I am in Hong Kong I stay with her. To her children from her two husbands, I am 'nana'— maternal grandfather.

Once having re-established contact with Ghayoor, I never lost it. Every time I go to Hyderabad, we spend our evenings together. She has become very frail and nearly blind. She has also become very religious. It is five prayers a day and a daily appeal to Allah to send for her. The last time I was in Hyderabad, I had to track her down to an old ladies' home.

She took me to a dargah where her parents

and sisters are buried. She has reserved a site for her own grave. 'I paid Rs 1,500 for it fifteen years ago. Today this would cost more than Rs 15,000', she told me. 'Why don't you sell it and make a profit?' I said trying to cheer her up. She turned down the suggestion.

'I have had salt sprinkled on the grave. It is a Hyderabadi custom, and no one else besides me can be buried there.'

As I was leaving, Ghayoor said, 'I have no one left in the world who bothers about me except you. Fareesa is involved with her own family and hardly ever writes to me. My parents and all my sisters are dead. Why does Allah not listen to my prayers and send for me? I don't want to live any longer.'

Sadia Dehlvi

It was in 1987 at Amina Ahuja's calligraphy exhibition, that I first met her. 'Come, let me introduce you to Sadia Dehlvi,' said Amina taking me by my hand and leading me to a girl sitting on a *morha* in the middle of a crowded room. The girl didn't bother to get up. She simply gaped at me with her large, luscious eyes. Her jet-black hair cascaded in curls around her oval face. There was nothing I could think of saying to her except blurting out, 'Why are you so beautiful?'

Her face flushed with joy as she put out her hand and replied, 'If you think I am beautiful, I must be beautiful', or words to that effect. I had not caught her name and asked her to tell me again. 'Sadia Dehlvi,' she replied. 'You must have heard of the Dehlvis of the Sharma group of journals. I am Yunus Dehlvi's daughter. I edit an Urdu magazine, *Bano*.'

I spent an hour talking to her. I invited her to my home to meet my family. From that day to the time she married Reza Parvez and left for Pakistan, Sadia remained my closest friend. Our age difference did not matter at all. Nor the fact that she came from a conservative Muslim family well-known in northern India and that I, an aged Sikh, was often described by the gutter press as the 'dirty old man of Delhi'. Although often seen with me, I meant to keep our friendship to ourselves. Not Sadia. She proclaimed from the house tops and in interviews to Bombay's gossip magazines that 'the only man in my life is Khushwant Singh.'

Sadia was emotionally very promiscuous. And utterly outspoken. She talked to me by the hour telling me of the many men in her life. She had made a disastrous marriage with the scion of a family that ran the leading Urdu daily in Calcutta. Her husband had been mother-fixated and prone to violence. She divorced him and returned to her parents' home. She was a restless character, ever changing her jobs and admirers. She would open a boutique one day, talk of the millions she would make in a few months and then close it after a few days to start a furniture business. She would take a franchise in a restaurant and give it up in a few days to make bigger millions by exporting carpets.

For a while she toyed with the idea of getting into politics. She led a march to Meerut where communal riots had broken out, and tried to nurse Jamia Nagar and Zakir Bagh which had sizeable Muslim populations, as her constituency. She went abroad a few times. Once in England she ran out of money and worked as a barmaid in a pub serving beer to customers. To atone for her 'sins', on her way back to India, she broke journey to perform an Umra pilgrimage at Mecca and Medina. She had a natural flair for writing, and was commissioned by *India Today* as well as *The Times of India* to write regular columns for them. No one could have asked for a bigger break. Her enthusiasm lasted a few weeks. She quickly got bored with anything she did. One time she took to riding and then decided to learn flying instead. She hired a *maulvi* sahib to teach her Persian and Arabic. Then the zest for living got the better of the desire to become a scholar. She loved animals and once bought a cuddly little cocker spaniel. Then one day she dumped it in the flat of her then closest girl friend, Kamna Prasad, promising to pick it up later that evening. Three days later Kamna had to deposit the pup in Sadia's home.

Sadia had a grasshopper's personality. Above everyone else, she loved herself. Once she was in the press party that accompanied Rajiv Gandhi on a foreign tour. Being much the most photogenic in the group next to the prime minister, she attracted more attention on television and in the media. For a while she toyed with the idea of joining the Congress party and getting into one or the other houses of Parliament, but soon got bored with the idea.

One thing Sadia was consistent about was wanting to get married. More than marriage, she wanted to be a mother. Her husband had to be Muslim. The father of her child had to be Muslim. When the late Ismat Chugtai advised her to be bold and produce a bastard ('*Haraamee paida kar*'), Sadia was appalled.

Many eligible men proposed marriage to her. She gave them *bhaav* but never her hand in marriage. Ultimately it was Reza Parvez, almost twenty years older than her, divorced father of two grown-up children and a Shia (Sadia is Sunni), who wore down Sadia's resistance. Her mother kept telling her right till the day of her wedding, that if she wanted to change her mind, she could do so before signing the *nikahnamah*. She did not change her mind. I signed the *nikahnamah* as a witness to her consent to marry Reza. I thought Sadia would take Pakistani citizenship and go out of my life. Once again I had misjudged her.

A few months after Sadia and Reza had settled down in Islamabad to what appeared to me blissful and happy matrimony, they came to meet me in Lahore where I had been invited to deliver the Manzur Qadir Memorial Lecture on Indo-Pak relations. Sadia came to the lecture dressed in a gorgeous sari. Pakistani women invariably wore salwar-kameez. Sadia sported a red bindi on her forehead. In Pakistan this was the sign of *kufr* (heresy) worn by infidels. She had become aggressively Indian in a country which regarded India as enemy number one. In course of time, a Pakistani rag denounced Sadia as an Indian spy. She became persona non grata in Pakistani society. Reza was fired from his job.

Sadia was confused and unhappy. Far from being a *Grihalakshmi*, she had brought misfortune on her husband's household. She was back in Delhi looking for a job and seeing gynaecologists wanting to know why she had not conceived. Reza, she confided to me, was a great lover. The couple returned to Pakistan. Reza had to sell his house in Karachi to keep the home fires burning. Slowly the wheel of fortune turned in their favour. Reza found a job; Sadia was pregnant. A son was born to them. They named him Armaan. Six months later Sadia brought Armaan to meet his real grandfather—me. She chided me for not having dedicated any book to her. So I did. *Not a Nice Man to Know* bears the dedication: 'To Sadia Dehlvi who gave me more affection and notoriety than I deserved.'

Anees Jung

If I had to draw a list of the most engaging conversationalists I have met in my life, Anees Jung's name would feature right at the top. Even though I am never sure that what she tells me is true or a figment of her fantasies.

She could flatter any man out of his wits, then run him down while talking to others. And if confronted, flatly deny having done so. She does it to me all the time and yet I look forward to being with her. She is a good hostess, serves gourmet food and vintage wines. She often has well-known singers to entertain her guests. She is an incorrigible name-dropper, but the amazing truth is that she does in fact know all the names she drops.

To her home come Presidents of the Republic, cabinet ministers, leaders of the Opposition, Governors, national figures, poets, writers, ambassadors and counsellors.

The paradigm for human beings according to her, is what she describes as the 'Renaissance gentleman': Well-dressed, sophisticated, *au courant* with the arts, literature and lifestyle. Her self-image is that of a Renaissance lady who gathers men around her. Where did I fit in her scheme of things?

Well, I was the first to give her a job. I have known her for over thirty years. And though often exasperated by her go-getting ways and saying nasty things about people behind their backs, I could never drop her. She took good care that I did not do so.

Sometime in the early 1960s, she returned with a degree from some American university. She rang up my wife to say that she had met our son in Bombay and he had suggested that she get in touch with his parents when she was in Delhi. She was promptly invited to lunch. Both of us were charmed by her. She bore an aristocratic, Hyderabadi name, 'Jung'.

She spoke English without a trace of an American accent and Hindustani in the *Dakkhani* lilt and the genders all mixed up which I find very attractive. She was looking for a job. I had a temporary one to offer. I was conducting a party of American students around the world. Two months were to be spent in India. We had completed one month in Delhi. The second was to be in Hyderabad. The boys and girls had to be put up with

Hyderabadi families and lectures arranged for them.

Anees was a Hyderabadi who knew the best families in the city. She accepted the job at what was then a handsome remuneration. She executed her assignment with dispatch and found excellent homes for all my students getting top academics like Professor Rashiduddin, MP, to speak to them. At the same time, instead of one Delhi-Hyderabad-Delhi air trip, she made me pay for three. She got under the skin of the family she was staying with and was unceremoniously thrown out. Far from being crushed, she bounced back to life and made her presence felt in the city.

Whenever she came to see me in any hotel, she drove up in the American Consul-General's big limousine. At a dinner reception hosted by this diplomat, she overshadowed all the others present. Many guests got the impression she was closely connected with the family of the Nizam of Hyderabad.

Actually, Anees Jung's ancestors were not from Hyderabad but from Lucknow. Her father, Hoshiar, migrated to Hyderabad and soon attracted the Nizam's attention. He was a very cultivated man with a gift for words. Though never formally given an official position, he was given the title 'Nawab', and became a very close companion *masahib* of His Exalted Highness and was granted a large haveli and other real estate in the city.

The family lived in feudal splendour till, for reasons unknown, he fell out of favour and lost most of what he had. Nothing now remains of Nawab Hoshiar Jung's wealth. However, Anees can be forgiven for believing that her father was a minister—even prime minister—of Hyderabad.

Being go-getting is Anees's second nature. Once when I was invited to Guwahati, a Canadian woman, Sue Dexter (over six feet tall), who wanted to see as much of India as she could in a fortnight, asked me if she could come along with me. I agreed that she could but warned her that I had many engagements in Guwahati and would not have much time to take her around. Also that she would have to find her own accommodation as I would be staying in the Circuit House. She asked Anees, whose sister she knew, to come along as her escort, all expenses paid. We arrived at Guwahati to a guard of honour presented by

the Khalsa High School and a band playing
the national anthem. The two women came
to the Circuit House with me. Sue Dexter
found a room in a small hotel. Anees rang up
the Governor, B.K. Nehru, and told him she
was a friend of his son and did not know
where to stay in Guwahati. She was invited to
stay at the Raj Bhavan.

For the next three days, the three of us
rode in the Governor's car to see the sights
along the Brahmaputra.

Her muscling in on President Zail Singh's
visit to Bombay to inspect the Indian Navy
was even more audacious. When I told her I
had been invited by Gianiji to accompany
him, she simply rang up Rashtrapati Bhavan
and told the President's secretary that she
would be coming along as well.

We flew in the President's private plane.
While I stayed in a hotel, Anees was a guest
of Governor Ali Yavar Jung. She flew back on
the same plane. President Zail Singh was
enchanted by her *bada gharana* upbringing
and impeccable manners. Every Eid, a
Presidential hamper of fruit was delivered at
her flat.

I had many opportunities of seeing Anees

Jung when I was editing *The Illustrated Weekly
of India*. The board of Bennett Coleman
wanted to launch a magazine for the young. I
was involved in the decision taken regarding
the choice of editor. I chose Anees Jung.
Youth Times was based in Delhi. But within a
few weeks Anees had become a great favourite
of the board, particularly with the general
manager, Mr Ram Tarneja.

She was in and out of Bombay whenever
she wished. Every evening she would be
seen sitting in the back of Tarneja's car parked
in the portico. All the staff going home viewed
her as the most privileged of editors of *The
Times of India* group of papers.

I was very put off and decided to have
nothing to do with her. For a couple of years
after being thrown out of *The Illustrated Weekly
of India*, I refused to speak to her. At a
reception in the house of the Pakistani High
Commissioner, she came to sit near me. I got
up and took another seat. 'So it is still like
that,' she remarked and went into a sulk.

Youth Times didn't survive. Anees was
once again out of a job. Then for the first
time she thought of doing some serious
writing. Everyone was surprised to find she

had a talent for good, straight and very
evocative writing. I don't recall how we got
together again, but she was with me when I
went to Amritsar in June 1984 to see the
havoc wrought by the Indian Army in
Operation Bluestar. It was not I, a Sikh, but
Anees Jung, a Shia Muslim, who kept making
offerings of flowers, money and prasaad at
every shrine we visited.

It would be unfair to describe Anees Jung
as *matlabee*, a seeker of favours. Her columns
in *The Times of India* gave her an all-India
readership. She has published many books
and *Unveiling India* went into many editions
opening up several avenues for her. She got a
lucrative assignment from the UN to do a
definitive book on the status of women in
Asia. It was released at the UN conference on
population in Cairo. She is currently with the
UNESCO and is a voice for Asian women.

I haven't met another woman quite like
Anees Jung, and I am tempted to write a
novel with her as the central character.

Kamna Prasad

It was sometime in 1980, soon after I had taken over the editorship of *The Hindustan Times*, that Kum Kum Chaddha who had become one of my favourites on the staff asked me, 'Sir, I want you to meet my closest friend. She wants to meet you.' (After fourteen years of visiting each other's homes and despite my protesting, Kum Kum continues to address me as 'Sir'. So does Kamna. She goes a step further. She never uses my name even when talking to third parties; it's always, 'Can I speak to Sir?')

The next day Kum Kum brought Kamna over to my office and left her there for us to get to know each other. I found her uncommonly beautiful in the classical Indian mould—like an Ajanta fresco.

She was a couple of inches taller than me. Long, lustrous, jet-black hair falling down to her hips. Neither very fair nor very dark, she has a light *café-au-lait* complexion. Beautiful neck, middle-sized bosom, very slender waist with her flat belly displaying her belly button and unusually broad hips designed to accommodate a brood of children.

I gathered that she was from Patna; her father was into Urdu poetry and she herself could quote Urdu and Hindi poetry fluently. Her mother had been a minister in the Bihar Government but due to poor health had retired from politics.

She was not very close to her parents but was devoted to her younger brother Raju. Her elder brother was married to Babu Jagjivan Ram's daughter but she rarely saw him.

She lived alone in Delhi and worked for a Gujarati firm engaged in the export of ready-made garments and semi-precious stones.

I did not get all these facts at the very first meeting. I gathered all this information after many sessions of interrogation because Kamna was a very private person and inexplicably secretive about small things.

I invited Kamna to come to my house with Kum Kum. I knew she had to have my wife's approval to become a regular visitor. She came and soon won over the affections of the entire family including our servants.

But it was only with me that she shared her confidences. Gradually, I became a father figure. She often sat on the floor beside my chair. I rested my hand on her silken-soft shoulders as she poured out her heart to me. She never opened up completely but always held something back for the next meeting.

Kamna had a way with people, both men and women, which drew them towards her. She was also very touchy about certain issues and took offence when no offence was meant. She was particularly sensitive about the fact that being attractive, living alone and in some style, she might give men the wrong idea about her availability.

She was often in our home in the evenings when drinks were served. I looked forward to her fixing my Scotch. Although a strict teetotaller, she knew how much was good for me. Once there were some other people present when I asked her to give me a drink and referred to her as my *saqi* (wine-server).

She was furious. She said nothing to me at the time but turned up the next day to berate me in no uncertain language. She accused me of having made her look like some kind of bimbo. I protested that I had used the word with affection as I had for Harjeet and Sadia who often saved me from having to pour my own Scotch and soda.

She remained unmoved and inconsolable. I apologised to her, but felt uneasy about the fact that if she could so utterly misunderstand my affection, our friendship would not last long. She forgave me and peace was restored.

Kamna became a favourite with my friends. But not everyone took to her.

Anees Jung could not understand why I liked Kamna and tried to dismiss her as a very lightweight person. Once when Anees and I had found ourselves together in Bombay in the same hotel with Kamna and Kum Kum in the adjoining room, Smita Patil, the celebrated film star, rang me up to say she wanted to see me.

As editor of *The Illustrated Weekly of India* I had put Smita on the cover after having watched her first film, and had referred to her as the actress of the future. Smita wanted to come over to thank me personally.

Anees happened to drop in and was determined to meet Smita. Kamna was equally determined to see to it that Smita saw me alone. A lively slanging match began between the two.

After ignoring Kamna's presence, Anees

abruptly turned to her and said, 'Why don't
you go back to your room?' Kamna snapped
back, 'Why should I? Why don't you leave Sir
alone? Smita does not want to meet you, she
wants to meet Sir.' I don't recall how the
tussle ended. Smita came, spent a few minutes
with us and departed. A few months later she
was dead.

Being, as I have said before, uncommonly
attractive and instinctively generous, Kamna
drew a lot of men and women to her. Women
came and went. First there was Kum Kum,
then a toughy called Chaudhry, then Sadia.

Men were more abiding. She had many
suitors. She kept them at a respectable
distance as she did want to marry and beget
children. She went through a half-hearted
engagement with a clean-shaven Sardar living
in Kuwait. It came to nothing as Kamna was
determined to live in India.

Then there was a German, unhappily
married and with two children. He fell
desperately in love with Kamna and promised
to divorce his wife to marry her.

Another engagement ceremony with
Hindu rites took place in her apartment. She
even spent a couple of weeks in Germany to

see how she would fit in as a *hausfrau*. She
returned to Delhi disillusioned and
disengaged.

She was drawn towards the painter M.F.
Husain and enjoyed the attention he paid
her. He made several portraits of her, and at
her persistence, made two of mine. Her
portraits, along with one of mine, decorate
her home.

Then he started to take her for granted.
She gave short shrift to him and refused to
talk to him. Husain pleaded with me to beg
her to forgive him. She did so at her own
terms. He dedicated his autobiography to her.
They are friends again.

Much as I loved Kamna, I wanted to see
her married and bear children. She eyed a
lovely, large painting in my home and asked
me to give it to her. 'I will give it to you as
a wedding present,' I told her. She took it
away without getting married. She liked a
large terracotta Ganesh that Anoop Sarkar
had given me. Again I promised to give it to
her as a wedding gift. And again she took it
without getting married.

When finally she did decide to get
married, she sprung it as a surprise. She asked

me over for a meal to meet a very special friend she had made. This was the tall, handsome, bearded Englishman Michael Battye of Reuters.

I could see with half an eye that he was deeply in love with Kamna and she with him. I had my doubts about their marriage as she knew nothing of his background or his career prospects. She left that part to me. I invited him over to see me. The next day I asked him what any father of a girl would like to know about his prospective son-in-law.

Michael had no private property nor much of a bank balance. He had good prospects of getting to the top in Reuters but that would involve many postings away from India and finally settling down in England.

I couldn't see Kamna, an elegant hostess, scrubbing floors, cooking and washing dishes in a flat in London's suburbs. A father-in-law-to-be should ask his son-in-law-to-be to produce a physical fitness certificate. That was too delicate a subject and Michael was not wanting in health and handsomeness.

I told Kamna I approved of him but was not sure if she could make a home in England. However, a marriage date was fixed. I agreed to perform *kanyadaan*.

I had to go to Assam to preside over a literacy conference at Sibsagar with assurance from Chief Minister Hiteshwar Saikia that he would get me back to Delhi in time for the nuptials. Indian Airlines decided otherwise. My flight from Calcutta to Delhi was delayed by six hours.

I returned home after the Hindu rites of the Kamna-Michael wedding were over. Kamna's parents had come over from Patna to give her away to her English groom.

A week later a civil marriage was performed in my apartment where Michael's parents were present. Rani Jethmalani and I signed the certificate as witnesses.

Kamna moved out of her spacious apartment to a more spacious bungalow rented by Reuters. She went to England with Michael, spent a few weeks with his parents and sister. They bought an apartment in Belsize Park in North London.

Even so, I could not reconcile myself to Kamna living anywhere else except Delhi and going out of my life forever.

I am unable to analyse my affection for Kamna. It is much more than her physical appearance. She is a giver, not a taker. For whatever I gave her (or she extracted from me), she returned twice over in gifts to my wife, daughter and granddaughter. Anything my wife wanted done, she could rely on Kamna to have it done, and with difficulty pay her the cost.

Perhaps the most important factor behind my affection for her was her faith and trust in me. I began to dread the day when Michael would get orders transferring him to some other country.

Without Kamna, Delhi would not be the same.

Amrita Shergil

I am hardly justified in describing Amrita
Shergil as a woman in my life. I met her only
twice. But these two meetings remain
imprinted in my memory. Her fame as an
artist, her glamour as a woman of great beauty
which she gave credence to in some of her
self-portraits, and her reputation for
promiscuity snowballed into a veritable
avalanche which hasn't ended to this day and
gives me an excuse to include her in my list.

One summer, her last, I heard that she
and her Hungarian cousin-husband who was a
doctor had taken an apartment across the road
where I lived in Lahore. He meant to set up
a medical practice; she, her painting studio.
Why they chose to make their home in Lahore,
I have no idea. She had a large number of
friends and admirers in the city. She also had
rich, landowning relatives on her Sikh father's
side who regularly visited Lahore. It seemed
as good a place for them to start their lives as
any in India.

It was June 1941. My wife had taken our
seven-month-old son, Rahul, for the summer

to my parents' house 'Sunderban' in Mashobra, seven miles beyond Simla. I spent my mornings at the High Court gossiping with lawyers over cups of coffee or listening to cases being argued before judges. I had hardly any case to handle myself. Nevertheless, I made it a point to wear my black coat, white tabs around the collar and carry my black gown with me to give others an appearance of being very busy. I returned home for lunch and a long siesta before I went to play tennis at the Cosmopolitan Club.

One afternoon I came home to find my flat full of the fragrance of expensive French perfume. On the table in my sitting room-cum-library was a silver tankard of chilled beer. I tiptoed to the kitchen, asked my cook about the visitor. 'A memsahib in a sari,' he informed me. He had told her I would be back any moment for lunch. She had helped herself to a bottle of beer from the fridge and was in the bathroom freshening up. I had little doubt my uninvited visitor was none other than Amrita Shergil.

For several weeks before her arrival in Lahore I had heard stories of her exploits during her previous visits to the city before

she had married her cousin. She usually stayed
in Faletti's Hotel. She was said to have made
appointments with her lovers with two-hour
intervals—at times six to seven a day—before
she retired for the night. If this was true
(men's gossip is less reliable than women's)
love formed very little part of Amrita's life.
Sex was what mattered to her. She was a
genuine case of nymphomania, and according
to her nephew Vivan Sundaram's published
account, she was also a lesbian. Her modus
vivendi is vividly described by Badruddin
Tyabji in his memoirs. One winter when he
was staying in Simla, he invited Amrita to
dinner. He had a fire lit for protection from
cold and Europian classical music playing on
his gramophone. He wasted the first evening
talking of literature and music. He invited
her again. He had the same log fire and the
same music. Before he knew what was
happening, Amrita simply took her clothes off
and lay stark naked on the carpet. She did not
believe in wasting time. Even the very proper
Badruddin Tyabji got the message.

Years later Malcolm Muggeridge, the
celebrated author, told me that he had spent
a week in Amrita's parents' home in Summer

Hill, Simla. He was then in the prime of his youth—his early twenties. In a week she had reduced him to a rag. 'I could not cope with her,' he admitted. 'I was glad to get back to Calcutta.'

A woman with the kind of reputation Amrita enjoyed drew men towards her like iron filings to a magnet. I was no exception. As she entered the room, I stood up to greet her. 'You must be Amrita Shergil,' I said. She nodded. Without apologizing for helping herself to my beer she proceeded to tell me why she had come to see me. They were mundane matters which robbed our first meeting of all romance. She wanted to know about plumbers, dhobis, carpenters, cooks, bearers etc. in the neighbourhood whom she could hire. While she talked I had a good look at her. Short, sallow-complexioned, black hair severely parted in the middle, thick sensual lips covered in bright red lipstick, stubby nose with blackheads visible. She was passably good looking but by no means a beauty.

Her self-portraits were exercises in narcissism. She probably had as nice a figure as she portrayed herself in her nudes but I had no means of knowing what she concealed beneath her sari. What I can't forget is her brashness. After she had finished talking, she looked around the room. I pointed to a few paintings and said, 'These are by my wife; she is an amateur.' She glanced at them and scoffed, 'That is obvious.' I was taken aback by her disdain but did not know how to retort. More was to come.

A few weeks later I joined my family in Mashobra. Amrita was staying with the Chaman Lals who had rented a house above my father's. I invited them for lunch. The three of them—Chaman, his wife Helen and Amrita, came at midday. The lunch table and chairs were lined on a platform under the shade of a holly oak which overlooked the hillside and a vast valley. My seven-month-old son was in the playpen teaching himself how to stand up on his feet. He was a lovely child with curly brown locks and large questioning eyes. Everyone took turns to talk to him and compliment my wife for producing such a beautiful boy. Amrita remained lost in the depths of her beer mug. When everyone had finished, she gave the child a long look and remarked, 'What an ugly little boy!' Everyone froze. Some protested at the unkind remark. But Amrita was back to drinking her beer. After our guests had departed, my wife said to me very firmly, 'I am not having that bloody bitch in my house again.'

Amrita's bad behaviour became the talk of Simla's social circle. So did my wife's comment on her. Amrita got to know what my wife had said and told people, 'I will teach that bloody woman a lesson she won't forget; I will seduce her husband.'

I eagerly awaited the day of seduction. It never came. We were back in Lahore in the autumn. So were Amrita and her husband. One night her cousin Gurcharan Singh (Channi) who owned a large orange orchard near Gujranwala turned up and asked if he could spend the night with us, as Amrita, who had asked him over for the weekend, was too ill to have him stay with her. The next day, other friends of Amrita's dropped in. They told us that Amrita was in a coma and her parents were coming down from Summer Hill to be with her. She was an avid bridge player and in her semi-conscious moments mumbled bridge calls. The next morning I heard that Amrita was dead.

I hurried to her apartment. Her father,

Sardar Umrao Singh Shergil, stood by the door in a daze, mumbling a prayer. Her Hungarian mother went in and out of the room where her daughter lay dead unable to comprehend what had happened. That afternoon no more than a dozen men and women followed Amrita's corètge to the cremation ground. Her husband lit her funeral pyre. When we returned to her apartment, the police were waiting for her husband. Britain had declared war on Hungary as an ally of its enemy, Nazi Germany. Amrita's husband was therefore considered an enemy because of his nationality, and had to be detained in prison.

He was lucky to be in police custody. A few days later, his mother-in-law, Amrita's mother, started a campaign against him accusing him of murdering her daughter. She sent letters to everyone she knew asking for a full investigation into the circumstances of her daughter's sudden death. I was one of those she sent a letter to. Murder it certainly was not; negligence, perhaps. I got details from Dr Raghubir Singh who was our family doctor and the last person to see Amrita alive. He told me that he had been summoned at midnight. Amrita had peritonitis caused perhaps by a clumsy abortion. She had bled profusely. Her husband asked Dr Raghubir Singh to give her blood transfusion. The doctor refused to do so without fully examining his patient. While the two doctors were arguing with each other, Amrita quietly slipped out of life. But her fame liveth evermore.

The Beggar Maid

For the first few months after taking over the editorship of *The Illustrated Weekly of India*, I lived as a paying guest of a young Parsi couple in a flat in Churchgate. I did not know many people, so had very little of a social life. I walked to the office every morning and walked back every evening as I refused to use the car and chauffeur provided for me.

Among the earliest friends I made was A.G. Noorani who combined practising law with journalism. He was and is, a bachelor. We began to spend our evenings together. We would go for a stroll along Marine Drive and return to my flat.

I had my evening ration of Scotch; Noorani, who was and is a teetotaller, had a glass of aerated water. Then we set off to try out different restaurants in the neighbourhood. After dinner we tried different *paanwalas* and bade each other good night. This routine was upset with the onset of the monsoon in Bombay. That's when I ran into the lady about whom I write.

There was a break in the downpour. I

was alone as I stepped out of a restaurant. A gas station and a few shops were on my way home. I stopped there to buy myself a *paan* and chatted with a bhelpuri*wala* and asked him how his business was during the rains. 'Not very well,' he admitted. '*Magar iski kismat jaag jatee hai* (her fortune increases),' he added pointing to a woman sitting on the steps of a shop nearby. 'What I can't sell, I give to her. She is a beggar. *Thori paagal hai* (she is a little mad).' I looked at the woman devouring bhelpuri. An uncommonly attractive girl, she was in her mid-twenties.

Fair, beautifully proportioned, uncombed hair wildly scattered about her face, a dirty white dhoti untidily draped around her body. I gazed at her for quite some time and wondered what an attractive young woman was doing alone in this vice-ridden city. I fantasized about her long into the night.

Thereafter, I made it a point to buy my after-dinner *paan* from the same *paanwala* by the gas station, exchange a few words with the bhelpuri*wala* as I ogled at the beggar maid on the steps of the closed shop. I often saw her talking to herself. I tried to buy bhelpuri to give to the girl, but the stall owner rejected my offer. He had plenty of leftovers, and feeding the girl was his monopoly.

One evening while I was at dinner, the clouds burst in all their fury and the roads around Churchgate were flooded. I tucked my trousers up to my knees, took my sandals in my hands, unfurled my umbrella to save my turban and waded through the swirling muddy water. Both the *paanwala* and the bhelpuri*wala* had shut shop and gone home. I saw the beggar girl stretched out on the marble steps barely an inch above the stream of rain water running past her. She couldn't have had anything to eat that night. I was sorely tempted to give her some money but was not sure how she would react. I walked home thinking about her, and again thought about her late into the night.

It poured all through the night. As I woke up to look out of the window that overlooked the maidan with the Rajabhai clock tower on the other side, the rain was still coming down in sheets. The maidan was flooded. I saw the shadowy figure of a woman walking across the maidan with a tin in her hand. I saw her hike her wet dhoti and start splashing water between her buttocks. I trained my field glasses on her. She turned to see whether anyone was around. Having reassured herself that she wasn't being watched, she took off her dhoti and stood stark naked in the pouring rain. It was my beggar woman. She poured dirty water on her body, rubbed her bosom, waist, arms and legs. The 'bath' over, she put the wet dhoti back on her and sloshed her way back towards Churchgate station.

The vision of Venus arising out of the sea in the form of a beggar maid of Bombay haunted me for the many days that I was away in Delhi. When I returned to Bombay I made it a point to go to Churchgate for my after-dinner stroll. The *paanwala* and the bhelpuri*wala* were there. But not the beggar. I asked the bhelpuri*wala* what had happened to the girl. His eyes filled with tears and his voice choked as he replied: '*Saaley bharooay utha ke lay gaye* (the bloody pimps abducted her).'

My Wife, Kaval

Most people who don't know me or my family are under the impression that my wife doesn't exist or that she is tucked away in some village like the wives of many of our *netas*. This is a grievous error, as my wife is quite a formidable character who rules the home with as firm a hand as Indira Gandhi ruled India. Unlike the mod girls of today who bob their hair, wear T-shirts, jeans and speak chi chi Hinglish, but when it comes to being married, tamely surrender their right to choose husbands to their parents, my wife made her own choice over sixty years ago.

I soon learnt that I could not take my wife for granted. If she did not like any of my friends, she told them so to their faces and in no uncertain terms. She is a stronger woman than any I have known. Her mother was very upset when she discovered that she drank whisky. One evening her mother stormed into the room, picked up her glass and threw it on the marble floor. The glass did not break but slithered across the floor, spilling its contents. My wife quickly picked it up and refilled it. 'I am an adult and a married woman. You have no right to dictate to me,' she told her mother. When her mother was suffering from cancer, she asked her to promise that she would say her prayers regularly. Despite my pleas to say 'yes' to her dying mother, she refused to do so. 'I will not make a promise that I know I will not keep.' She nursed her mother for many months, sitting with her head in her lap and pressing it all through the nights. She was with her when she died. She took her bath and went to the coffee house to have her breakfast. When some friends asked her about her mother's health she replied, 'She is okay.' She then came home and told the servants that she would not receive any visitors who came to condole with her. She did not shed a tear. She did not go to her mother's funeral or any of the religious ceremonies that followed. On the other hand, when our dog Simba fell ill, she sat all night stroking him. When he died at the ripe old age of fourteen, she was heartbroken.

The rigid discipline of time maintained in our home is entirely due to my wife. I have only recently taught myself how to speed the

departure of long-winded visitors. She has
always given short shrift to them. No one
drops in on us without prior warning. If any
relation breezes in in the morning, she ignores
his or her presence and continues with her
housework and decides the menus for the
day. (We eat the most gourmet meals—
French, Chinese, Italian, South Indian and
occasionally Punjabi. She has two shelves full
of cookery books which she consults before
discussing the meals with our cook Chandan,
who has been with us for over thirty years.)
Or she continues to teach the servants'
children and help them with their homework.
We don't accept lunch or tea invitations nor
offer them. When we have people over for
dinner, no matter who they are, whether
cabinet ministers or ambassadors, they are
reminded to be punctual and told that we do
not expect our guests to stay after 9 p.m.
Once the German ambassador and his wife
had come over. The meal was finished at 8.30
p.m. Liqueurs were served. It was 8.45 p.m.
The Ambassador took out his cigar and asked
my wife, 'I know, Mrs Singh, that you like
your guests to leave before 9 p.m., but can I
have my cigar before we go?' My wife

promptly replied, 'I am sure Mr Ambassador, you will enjoy it more in your car.' He laughed and stood up saying, 'I get it.' And departed without any rancour.

I have a lot of pretty girls visiting me. They are dead scared of my wife and know that they have to be on her right side to keep dropping in. All of them take good care never to offend her.

Why do so few people know about my wife? She is allergic to photographers and pressmen. All you have to do is take out your camera, tape recorder or pen and she will order you out of the house. The allergy runs in the women in the family. My daughter and granddaughter react the same way.

It was during my stay in Welwyn Garden in my first year in England, that I ran into a girl, Kaval Malik, who had been with me at Modern School. She had always been a good-looking, light-skinned girl and a bit of a tomboy, playing hockey and soccer with the boys. When I left school, she was still a gawky girl, a couple of years my junior. I had lost track of her when I moved to Lahore. When I ran into her in England, she had blossomed into a beauty and was much sought

after by many boys I knew, some from India's
richest families. Her parents were orthodox
Sikhs and were determined to marry her off
to a Sikh boy in the Civil Services. They
stood in awe of the Indian Civil Service, and
her uncle, who had made it, was worshipped
as a hero. At the time, they were negotiating
with parents of Sikh boys sitting for
competitive exams. Meeting the girl now
grown into a young lady caused me anguish,
as I fell desperately in love with her and also
felt that I stood little chance of winning her.
Amongst other obstacles was the fact that her
father was a senior engineer in the Public
Works Department, while mine was a builder
who had to get contracts from the same.
Besides, I was studying law, and lawyers,
being a dime a dozen, were poorly rated in
the marriage market. Her parents thought
well of me, as a year earlier they had visited
me in my lodgings. Her mother had found
the Sikh prayer book under my pillow and
had been deeply impressed. I met them again
in the Lake District. They were staying in a
fancy hotel at Bowness; I, in a lodging house
at Windermere. I rowed up seven miles to
have breakfast with them. I knew they would

agree to their daughter marrying me if they could not find a better Sikh proposal.

My best chance was to bypass the parents and approach the girl directly. The Christmas vacations were near and she had nowhere to go. I suggested that she come with me to the Quaker hostel in Buckinghamshire. She wrote to her parents to seek their permission. To my utter surprise, they agreed that she could go. I began courting her as soon as the train left London. And continued paying court throughout our fortnight's stay with the Quakers. On our way back to London, I asked her if I could ask my parents to approach hers with the proposal. She nodded her consent.

Our engagement was announced a few days later. It caused a lot of heartache amongst her many suitors. A particularly ardent one, whose sister was married to my fiancee's brother, said very acidly, 'the bank balance won.' By that time, my father was known to be a man of considerable wealth. Though most of them envied me, the only one to try to dissuade me from marrying the girl was my closest friend, E.N. Mangat Rai, who, at the time, had a poor opinion of her. He was later

to fall deeply in love with her and almost
succeed in wrecking our marriage.

It took me a year more than prescribed to
take my bachelor of law degree, and I became
a Barrister-at-Law of the Inner Temple. In
the meantime, I had sat for the Indian Civil
Service exam. Rating my chances as negligible,
I had not taken one paper. When the results
were declared, I discovered to my great
surprise that I had just missed getting in. I
was the only candidate, English or Indian, to
be given full marks in the viva voce. I must
have impressed the interview board more
than the examiners of my papers.

I returned home by sea in the summer of
1939. There was talk of war breaking out. By
the time I reached Delhi, German armies had
been launched on their conquest of
neighbouring countries.

In October 1939, I got married. It was a
grand affair. My wife's father was by then
chief engineer of the PWD, the first Indian to
rise to the position. My father was
acknowledged as the biggest owner of real
estate in Delhi. We lived in a large stone and
marble mansion with over a dozen bedrooms,
a teak-panelled library, and chandeliered living

and dining rooms. At our wedding reception there were over fifteen hundred guests, including M.A. Jinnah, founding father of Pakistan. Champagne flowed like the Jamuna in flood. My wife received presents which, even after fifty years of being given away, were not exhausted. My father gave me a new car and rented an apartment and office space for me near the High Court in Lahore. And after a short honeymoon at Mount Abu in Rajasthan, the two of us drove to Lahore in our new Ford.

The Sardarji and the Starlet

I have two theories that I wish to illustrate through this almost entirely true short story. The first is that God compensates women He does not endow with good looks, in His own mysterious ways. A plain-looking, homely-type of girl need not envy her better-looking sisters because men are more likely to make passes at her than at girls who resemble Marilyn Monroe. He makes good-looking lasses haughty and arrogant and only gigolo types have the confidence to approach them. That is why the plainer-looking have a better time with men and end up making better marriages than pretty ones who seldom have a satisfying sex life and usually make disastrous marriages.

The second theory is somewhat hackneyed: Only the brave deserve the fair; equally well expressed in the maxim, 'Nothing ventured, nothing gained.'

Some thirty years ago, I was living in a two-bedroom basement flat in Highgate, London. I had recently resigned from the diplomatic service but still had my large

American limousine with a CD numberplate and a sizeable stock of duty-free champagne, Scotch, wines and liquors. My family had returned to India and I had three months of freedom to finish a book I was working on and whatever else I wanted to do in the way of keeping myself amused. The apartment above mine was occupied by a stenotyping agency that closed in the evening. The one above the agency was occupied by a young lady who, I was told, was a stage actress. She went to work late in the evening and returned home after the second show sometime after midnight. All three flats had one entrance. Since the only garage attached to the premises was too small to house my limousine, it was parked outside the entrance. The only source of natural light for my basement flat was a large window, half of which was above ground level alongside a bus stop. Sitting in my armchair I could see the legs of people queueing up outside or alighting from buses.

I spent most of the day working on my book. In the evenings, a girl who had been my secretary at India House came to collect whatever I had scribbled during the day and have tea with me before she departed. After

she left, I took a walk round Hampstead
Heath and returned home to light a fire,
drink, listen to music, eat a sandwich supper
and read till I felt sleepy. This was rarely
before midnight. And soon I began to time
my retirement with the sound of the opening
of the entrance door and the footsteps of the
actress-girl going up the stairs to her
apartment.

It was a few days later that I discovered
her identity. The lady who came to clean my
flat also did the other two apartments. One
morning I casually asked her about the
occupant of the top flat. 'That be Miss
Dawson,' she replied, 'Jennifer Dawson, pretty
as a picture she is. And very very nice too.
She gave me two free tickets to her show.
She's got a very small role. But mark my
words, she'll go far. One day I'll be proud of
having worked for her.'

Thereafter I kept a lookout for the last
bus which stopped by my apartment. And
soon got to recognize the pair of shapely legs
that alighted and then took their owner up
the steps.

One Sunday morning I contrived to make
her acquaintance. I had noted that she went

to the mid-morning service, and since there was no show on Sundays, spent the afternoons at home, presumably washing her clothes. As soon as I heard her footsteps coming down, I came out of my apartment. She extended her hand and said, 'We are neighbours but we have never met. I am Jennifer Dawson. Mrs Markham has told me you are Mr Singh. Nice to meet you.'

I took her proffered hand and replied, 'Mrs Markham told me you were pretty, but not *how* pretty you were. I am honoured living beneath a famous actress.'

'Famous my foot!' she said with a laugh. 'I am only a miserable extra. If you want to see how extra I am, I will be happy to give you a ticket for the show. That's the only thing I can afford; I get it free.'

I opened the front door for her and asked, 'Can I drop you anywhere? I have nothing much to do except take my car for an airing.'

She looked at my chariot-sized limousine. 'Cor blimey! Must drink up gas by the gallon! I am going to the church round the corner, I don't mind being driven in your American Rolls-Royce.'

I dropped her at the church. 'I can pick

you up on my way back; how long will the
service last?' I asked.

'You are most kind!' she replied. 'I should
be through in an hour. Sure you don't mind?'

'On this fine Sabbath morning I have
nothing whatsoever to do save eat the English
air. Allah is in His heaven and all's right with
the world.'

I went back to my apartment to freshen
up and was back outside the church. I switched
on the radio. I was lucky. It was Beethoven's
Ninth Symphony, the only piece of Western
classical music I was familiar with. It was
coming across in all its mellifluous beauty.

She was among the first to step out of the
church. She shook hands with the vicar and
ran towards the car. She certainly was a beauty:
hazel-brown hair tumbling down on her
shoulders, broad forehead, large brown eyes,
lovely neck and as shapely a figure as you
would see in a Miss Universe beauty contest.
Beethoven's magic worked. 'Let's not go home
till the symphony is over,' she pleaded.

I drove slowly round the heath, along
Spaniard's Inn Road and the Vale of Heath.
She kept humming softly to herself and tossing
her head to the music, completely oblivious

of my presence. We were passing Keats' Grove when the symphony reached its climactic end. 'That was wonderful,' she sighed. 'Thank you ever so much for indulging me. I have wasted all your precious morning.'

'It was a pleasure,' I replied. 'I wish you would waste more of them. I get awfully lonely having no one to talk to except Mrs Markham and my secretary for a few minutes every day. The rest of the time, it is books. And silence.'

She did not rise to the bait. Nor accept my invitation to have a bite with me before she went up. 'Who will do all my laundry and ironing, write my weekly letter to Ma and cook my supper? Thanks for a wonderful time,' she patted me on the shoulder and ran upstairs.

Next Sunday I slipped a note under her door inviting her for a drink in the evening after she had done her Sunday chores. She did not send a reply but as it turned dark and the street lights came on, I heard her footsteps come down the stairs and a gentle tap on my door. I leapt up from my chair to welcome her. 'It is very thoughtful of you to have invited me,' she said. She looked around the

dimly-lit room with only one table lamp above
my armchair. I switched on the room light
and went to help her take off her overcoat.
'It's freezing cold. Don't mind if I keep it
on?' she asked.

Mrs Markham always laid coal in the
grate. I took a bottle of gin and splashed it
over the heap and threw a lighted match on
it. The grate exploded into a blue flame and
soon we had a blazing fire going. 'How
extravagant can one be!' she exclaimed.
'Never heard of anyone lighting fire with
gin.'

'Duty-free diplomatic privilege,' I replied.
'Costs me very little and is quicker than
newspapers or wood chips. What would you
like, Scotch, sherry, gin, vodka, champagne?'

She slipped her overcoat off her shoulders
and warmed her hands before the grate. 'If
you are flush with liquor, I would not mind
some champagne,' she replied.

I got a bottle of Mouton Rothschild from
the freezer, uncorked it with professional skill
and poured the frothing, bubbling liquor into
the best cut glasses I had. I raised mine and
proposed the toast, 'To the most beautiful
girl in the world!' Her face flushed with

pleasure as she raised her glass and replied,
'To the world's nicest old man and the greatest
liar.'

She curled up in an armchair and sipped
champagne; I replenished her glass several
times. The fire in the grate glowed on her
face and lit the curls in her hair. 'Jennifer, you
must have lots of admirers and boyfriends,' I
said.

'Why do you say that?' she asked.

'Now you are fishing. Your mirror must
tell you why, every time you look into it.'

'You are nice!' she replied. 'Believe it or
not, I have never had any boyfriends.
Admirers, yes. A few. They pay me
compliments. And that's that.'

I paid her more compliments. Quoted
lines I knew of English poets in praise of
beautiful women. She listened with a distant
look in her eyes gazing into the embers of
coal glowing in the grate. I put on music. She
shut her eyes.

I made sandwiches and coffee and brought
them on a tray for her. I gently tapped her on
the shoulder. 'Asleep?'

She woke with a start. 'Not really. Day-
dreaming to the music. I should have been

doing all that, not you,' she said looking at the tray. 'You are spoiling me.'

We ate our sandwiches and drank our coffee in silence. I felt her questioning large eyes fixed on me. Could I dare make an advance? No, she was too beautiful for the likes of me and I did not want to lose her friendship by taking a false step. After a while she stood up. 'I don't want to go but I must drag myself away. Beauty sleep and all that— can't afford to look dowdy on the stage.' She gave me a peck on my nose. 'Thank you for a wonderful, wonderful evening.' She left and shut the door behind her.

I had established a rapport, proved that I was a gentleman who would not take unwelcome liberties with her. The rest I would leave to time. And her. I changed my working hours to suit hers.

Every night she came back from the theatre, I had the fire lit, a bottle of champagne in the freezer, sandwiches on a tray and a steaming pot of hot coffee. She had her night-cap with me. We spent our Sundays together. She told me that she went to church because she had nothing better to do and much preferred to drive out to the country, walk in

the woods and end the Sabbath by my fireside.
We did Kenwood and Kew, Burnham Beeches
and the Cotswolds and Stratford-on-Avon. I
got no closer to her than I had on the first
evening.

Then an old friend from my college days
in Lahore arrived in London. He had very
little money and gratefully accepted my
invitation to stay with me. He was a small,
effeminate Sardarji whose chief qualification
was being a good listener. No one would
suspect him of a being a ladies' man or regard
him as a rival. I told him about Jennifer, her
goddess-like aloofness, and cautioned him to
treat her with respect.

The first time they met he was on his
best behaviour. She gave him a ticket for her
show. They came back together. I was happy
they had hit it off. The following Sunday I
asked a few Indian friends we had known in
Lahore and their wives, for drinks. Needless
to say, Jennifer was the main attraction. And
a great success. She played the hostess and
talked to all the women. From the way my
guests looked at me I could sense that they
felt Jennifer was my woman and that I had
something very good going for me while my

family was away. I did not want to disabuse
them.

The party went on late into the night
with vast quantities of Scotch and champagne
going down their gullets. Everyone was in
high spirits, particularly my house guest who
took more than his share of liquor. Around
midnight, the guests departed, leaving Jennifer
and the Sardarji with me. They relaxed in
their armchairs while I removed empty glasses
and ashtrays. My Sardarji friend planted
himself on the carpet beside Jennifer's feet,
looking soulfully at her with his large cocker-
spaniel eyes. He rested his head against her
thighs and began stroking her shapely legs.

'Please tell your friend to behave himself,'
said Jennifer to me. I spoke to him in Punjabi.
He was too far gone to listen to me in any
language. Jennifer got up from her chair and
sat down in another. After a while, the Sardarji
hauled himself up, planted himself on the
arm of the same chair and began stroking
Jennifer's hair. I spoke more sharply this time.
It was of no use. 'Jennifer, I think you should
go to your apartment,' I suggested.

Jennifer only changed her chair. The
Sardarji followed her and resumed his

ministrations. I lost my temper. 'For God's sake, stop pestering Jennifer! You are drunk. You had better go to bed.'

He took no notice of me. It became like a game of hide-and-seek between the two, with me playing the role of a referee.

Neither took my advice to retire to their respective beds. Then in the game of chase, the Sardarji slipped and fell. His turban came off and he was sick all over my carpet. I was very angry, Jennifer apologized and left. I went off to my bedroom and left my house guest wallowing in his vomit.

The next morning I told my Sardarji friend to find lodgings elsewhere. He left without protest or apology. I wrote a note to Jennifer, apologizing for his behaviour and hoping that she would not drop me because of what had happened. I thought it best not to leave my door open to welcome her when she returned from the theatre, and instead let her, if she wanted, knock at my door. I found a note from her telling me not to worry. But she did not knock at my door. Night after night I saw her legs as she alighted from the bus, heard the click of the lock opening the front door and her footsteps going up the stairs. I felt let down and punished for no fault of mine. And lonely. I could not concentrate on my work. My peace of mind was gone. I felt that if I met my Sardarji friend again, I would punch him in the nose for what he had done by ruining a beautiful friendship.

Came next Sunday. Bright and sunny with peals of church bells from distant spires, the loudest being from 'Jennifer's "round the corner" '. I could not contain myself any more. I decided to go up to her bed-sitting room apartment—she had never invited me—and take her out for a drive into the country as we had done in the past. I was sure she would relent and make up.

I went up the dark stairway to the top floor. Beside the doorbell was a strip of paper with the name 'Jennifer Dawson' on it. I rang the bell. I heard Jennifer's voice shouting, 'See who it is! May be a telegram or something.' The door opened. Facing me stood my Sardarji friend in his pyjamas.

Lady Mohan Lal

Sir Mohan Lal looked at himself in the mirror of a first class waiting room at the railway station. The mirror was obviously made in India. The red oxide on its back had come off at several places and long lines of translucent glass cut across its surface. Sir Mohan smiled at the mirror with an air of pity and patronage.

'You are so very much like everything else in this country; inefficient, dirty, indifferent,' he murmured.

The mirror smiled back at Sir Mohan.

'You are a bit of all right, old chap,' it said. 'Distinguished, efficient—even handsome. That neatly-trimmed moustache, the suit from Saville Row with the carnation in the buttonhole, the aroma of eau de Cologne, talcum powder and scented soap all about you! Yes, old fellow, you are a bit of all right.'

Sir Mohan threw out his chest, smoothed his Balliol tie for the umpteenth time and waved a goodbye to the mirror.

He glanced at his watch. There was still time for a quick one.

'Koi Hai!'

A bearer in white livery appeared through a wire gauze door.

'Ek Chota,' ordered Sir Mohan, and sank into a large cane chair to drink and ruminate.

Outside the waiting room, Sir Mohan Lal's luggage lay piled along the wall. On a small grey steel trunk Lachmi, Lady Mohan Lal, sat chewing a betel leaf and fanning herself with a newspaper. She was short and fat and in her mid-forties. She wore a dirty white sari with a red border. On one side of her nose glistened a diamond nose pin, and she had several gold bangles on her arms. She had been talking to the bearer until Sir Mohan had summoned him inside. As soon as he had gone, she hailed a passing railway coolie.

'Where does the zenana stop?'

'Right at the end of the platform.'

The coolie flattened his turban to make a cushion, hoisted the steel trunk on his head, and moved down the platform. Lady Lal picked up her brass tiffin carrier and ambled along behind him. On the way she stopped by a hawker's stall to replenish her silver betel leaf case, and then joined the coolie. She sat down on her steel trunk (which the coolie had put down) and started talking to him.

'Are the trains very crowded on these lines?'

'These days all trains are crowded, but you'll find room in the zenana.'

'Then I might as well get over the bother of eating.'

Lady Lal opened the brass carrier and took out a bundle of cramped chapattis and some mango pickle. While she ate, the coolie sat opposite her on his haunches, drawing lines in the gravel with his finger.

'Are you travelling alone, sister?'

'No, I am with my master. He is in the waiting room. He travels first class. He is a vizier and a barrister, and meets so many officers and Englishmen on the trains—and I am only a native woman. I can't understand English and don't know their ways, so I keep to my zenana inter-class.'

Lachmi chatted away merrily. She was fond of a little gossip and had no one to talk to at home. Her husband never had any time to spare for her. She lived in the upper storey of the house, and he, on the ground floor. He did not like her poor illiterate relatives hanging about his bungalow, so they never came. He came up to her once in a while at night and stayed for a few minutes. He just ordered her about in anglicized Hindustani, and she obeyed passively. These nocturnal visits had, however, borne no fruit.

The signal came down and the clanging of the bell announced the approaching train. Lady Lal hurriedly finished off her meal. She got up, still licking the stone of the pickled mango. She emitted a long, loud belch as she went to the public tap to rinse her mouth and wash her hands. After washing she dried her mouth and hands with the loose end of her sari, and walked back to her steel trunk, belching and thanking the gods for the favour of a filling meal.

The train steamed in. Lachmi found herself facing an almost empty inter-class zenana compartment next to the guard's van at the tail end of the train. The rest of the train was packed. She heaved her squat, bulky frame through the door and found a seat by the window. She produced a two-anna bit from a knot in her sari and dismissed the coolie. She then opened her betel case and made herself two betel leaves charged with a

red and white paste, minced betel nuts and
cardamoms. These she thrust into her mouth
till her cheeks bulged on both sides. Then
she rested her chin on her hands and sat
gazing idly at the jostling crowd on the
platform.

The arrival of the train did not disturb Sir
Mohan Lal's sangfroid. He continued to sip
his Scotch and ordered the bearer to tell him
when he had moved the luggage to a first
class compartment. Excitement, bustle, and
hurry were exhibitions of bad breeding, and
Sir Mohan was eminently well bred. He
wanted everything 'ticketyboo' and orderly.
In his five years abroad, Sir Mohan had
acquired the manners and attitudes of the
upper classes. He rarely spoke Hindustani.
When he did, it was like an Englishman's—
only the very necessary words, and properly
anglicized. But he fancied his English, finished
and refined at no less a place than the
University of Oxford. He was fond of
conversation, and like a cultured Englishman,
he could talk on almost any subject—books,
politics, people. How frequently had he heard
English people say that he spoke like an
Englishman!

Sir Mohan wondered whether he would be travelling alone. It was a Cantonment and some English officers might be on the train. His heart warmed at the prospect of an impressive conversation. He never showed any sign of eagerness to talk to the English as most Indians did. Nor was he loud, aggressive and opinionated like them. He went about his business with an expressionless matter-of-factness. He would retire to his corner by the window and get out a copy of *The Times*. He would fold it in a way in which the name of the paper was visible to others while he did the crossword puzzle. *The Times* always attracted attention. Someone would like to borrow it when he put it aside with a gesture signifying 'I've finished with it.' Perhaps someone would recognize his Balliol tie which he always wore while travelling. That would open a vista leading to a fairyland of Oxford colleges, masters, dons, tutors, boat races and rugger matches. If both *The Times* and the tie failed, Sir Mohan would 'Koi Hai!' his bearer to get the Scotch out. Whisky never failed with Englishmen. Then followed Sir Mohan's handsome gold cigarette case filled with English cigarettes. English cigarettes in India?

How on earth did he get them? Sure he didn't mind? And Sir Mohan's understanding smile—of course he didn't. But could he use the Englishman as a medium to commune with his dear old England? Those five years of grey bags and gowns, of sports blazers and mixed doubles, of dinners at the Inns of Court and nights with Piccadilly prostitutes. Five years of a crowded glorious life. Worth far more than the forty-five in India with his dirty, vulgar countrymen, with sordid details of the road to success, of nocturnal visits to the upper storey and all-too-brief sexual acts with obese old Lachmi smelling of sweat and raw onions.

Sir Mohan's thoughts were disturbed by the bearer announcing the installation of the Sahib's luggage in a first class coupé next to the engine. Sir Mohan walked to his coupé with a studied gait. He was dismayed. The compartment was empty. With a sigh he sat down in a corner and opened the copy of *The Times* he had read several times before.

Sir Mohan looked out of the window down the crowded platform. His face lit up as he saw two English soldiers trudging along, looking in all the compartments for room.

They had their haversacks slung behind their backs and walked unsteadily. Sir Mohan decided to welcome them, even though they were entitled to travel only second class. He would speak to the guard.

One of the soldiers came up to the last compartment and stuck his face through the window. He surveyed the compartment and noticed the unoccupied berth.

''Ere, Bill,' he shouted, 'one 'ere.'

His companion came up, also looked in, and looked at Sir Mohan.

'Get the nigger out,' he muttered to his companion.

They opened the door, and turned to the half-smiling, half-protesting Sir Mohan.

'Reserved!' yelled Bill.

'*Janta*—Reserved.   Army—Fauj,' exclaimed Jim, pointing to his khaki shirt.

'*Ek dum jao*—get out!'

'I say, I say, surely,' protested Sir Mohan in his Oxford accent. The soldiers paused. It almost sounded like English, but they knew better than to trust their inebriated ears. The engine whistled and the guard waved his green flag.

They picked up Sir Mohan's suitcase and

flung it onto the platform. Then followed his thermos flask, briefcase, bedding and *The Times*. Sir Mohan was livid with rage.

'Preposterous, preposterous,' he shouted, hoarse with anger. 'I'll have you arrested— guard, guard!'

Bill and Jim paused again. It did sound like English, but it was too much of the King's for them.

'Keep yer ruddy mouth shut!' And Jim struck Sir Mohan flat on the face.

The engine gave another short whistle and the train began to move. The soldiers caught Sir Mohan by the arms and flung him out of the train. He reeled backwards, tripped on his bedding, and landed on the suitcase.

'Toodle-oo!'

Sir Mohan's feet were glued to the earth and he lost his speech. He stared at the lighted windows of the train going past him in quickening tempo. The tail end of the train appeared with a red light and the guard standing in the open doorway with the flags in his hands.

In the inter-class zenana compartment was Lachmi, fair and fat, on whose nose the diamond nose pin glistened against the station

lights. Her mouth was bloated with betel
saliva which she had been storing up to spit
as soon as the train had cleared the station. As
the train sped past the lighted part of the
platform, Lady Lal spat and sent a jet of red
dribble flying across like a dart.

Martha Stack

'This is Martha—Martha Stack. Do you remember me? We were together in Paris thirty years ago.' The voice was creamy: unmistakably Black American.

'Martha!' shouted Bannerjee enthusiastically into the mouthpiece.

'Of course I remember you! What on earth are you doing in Delhi? Why didn't you let me know you were coming?'

'Didn't know myself till the last minute before the plane left New York. But here I am at the Ashoka. Simply dying to see you again.'

'One moment Martha!' He put the palm of his hand on the mouthpiece, spoke to his wife, and resumed the dialogue. 'Come for dinner and meet the family.'

'Love to! Didn't know you had a family.'

'Wife and grown-up children. Boy, twenty; girl, fifteen. It's been a long time you know—thirty years! What about you?'

'No family no more. I've run through two husbands. Am by myself now.' she laughed. 'Much nicer.'

'I'll call for you at seven. I hope you will
be able to recognize me, I've gone somewhat
grey and fat.'

'Don't worry honey, we all get old and
fat,' she replied. 'See you around seven.
Namaste. Haven't forgotten that.'

Bannerjee put down the receiver. He
tried to look bored. His wife put him out of
countenance. 'Old girl friend?' she asked with
a smile.

'No girl friend. A woman I met at the
Sorbonne thirty years ago.'

'That's not what you told me first! Isn't
she the one in your album? Must be quite a
smasher.'

'Wasn't too bad to look at; but negroid.
Thick lips, fuzzy hair, that sort of thing. We
were the only coloured students in the class,
so we were sort of thrown together.'

He realized his voice did not ring true.
He avoided his wife's eyes. 'I'll have to fetch
her from the Ashoka,' he announced and
went back to his study.

Odd, he said to himself, thirty years ago
he had tried to impress his friends with his
association with Martha. He had her
photograph in his album. The picture of the

attractive Black girl in a large straw hat worn at a coquettish angle, with the inscription, 'Love, Martha' invariably aroused curiosity. 'And who is Martha?' his friends thumbing through the album would ask. 'Ask no questions and you'll hear no lies,' he would answer with a smile. And now he had to pretend that she had been little more than an acquaintance. That's what marriage does to people; they have to lie about the most innocent of relationships.

Innocent? Well, almost. His mind went back to the vacation term lectures on 'Literature Francais pour les Strangers' at the Sorbonne. There were about thirty boys and girls in the class—mostly American with a sprinkling of Dutch and Scandinavian. He and Martha were the only coloured students in the group.

Martha attracted attention from the very first day. She sat away from the others. She was taller than most of the men, coloured and uncommonly attractive. On the second day some boys introduced themselves to her and sat beside her. On the third, she came up to Bannerjee. 'Do you mind if I sit next to you? I am Martha Stack, I am American,' she said holding out her hand. 'My name is Bannerjee,' he replied half standing up, 'I am from India.'

Thereafter they had sat together in the class.

Bannerjee was usually an early arriver. He put his notebook on the seat beside him to indicate that it was 'taken'. He waited for Martha. Her receding hairline and fuzzy hair showed above the stream of students coming in. She walked slowly, her hips swayed rhythmically. She dropped gently into the seat beside Bannerjee. 'And how are we this morning? For God's sake, don't get up each time you see me.' The fragrance of jasmine spread about her. Why hadn't her parents named her 'Yasmeen'? Such a pretty name and much more appropriate than 'Martha'. During the lessons, Bannerjee's eyes would stray to his neighbour—her broad, powerful wrist adorned with a bracelet of gold coins which jingled as she wrote; her dark brown arms, and then her breasts, large for her bony frame but taut as unripe mangoes. When she went out, Bannerjee watched her slender form and swinging buttocks.

Bannerjee's admiration remained impersonal till the boys began to tease him.

'You lucky blighter! You're the only one she seems to notice.' But Bannerjee could not bring himself to make a pass at her. She was too tall for him. Her dress was too loud; if he took her out, people were bound to comment. In any case, it was a bit silly to come all the way to Europe and bed a woman blacker than yourself!

Martha took the initiative. One morning as they were walking out of the class together, she asked him casually, 'Care to join me for a cup of coffee?' And after the coffee when the waiter came for the bill and Bannerjee fumbled in his pocket, she took a firm grip of his wrist. 'No you don't! *I* asked you, *I* pay. When you take me out, I'll let you do it.' She kept her hand on his wrist till the waiter had taken the money from her. Bannerjee felt compelled to ask her out again. Thereafter, they had coffee together every day. Martha insisted on paying on alternate days. But this did not prevent Bannerjee from putting his hand in his pocket; nor Martha from holding it and saying, 'No Sir, it's my turn.'

Martha took the second step. 'For God's sake stop calling me Miss Stack! I am Martha. What's your first name?'

'My real name is Hiren but at home they call me Gulloo.'

Martha pressed his hand warmly. 'You're Gulloo to me.'

Bannerjee told her that he had given her an Indian name. And once again Martha pressed his hand and said, 'That's sweet! I like Yasmeen. And you are going to be the only one in the world to call me by that name.' She came close to him; he felt her breath on his forehead and caught a whiff of the negroid smell he had heard his friends talk of. He found it pleasant—warm and sexy. Much nicer than the sour-milk smell of the white women.

'Suppose I should get back to my French verbs: *J'aime, vous aime, nous aimons* . . .' She laughed and turned away.

Bannerjee wasted many hours day-dreaming about the way he would seduce Martha. And yet every time she gave him an opening, he withdrew into himself. Only ten days remained for the end of term.

Martha gave him yet another chance. 'Last weekend!' she exclaimed with a sigh. 'So it is,' replied Bannerjee laconically. 'How time flies!' Martha seemed determined to force the pace. 'Let's go some place; we may never meet again,' she pleaded. 'Let's get out into the open country,' suggested Martha. 'Somewhere up the Seine where we could bathe and lie in the sun.'

It was a hot, sunny day in August. They took an early morning train out of Paris. It was practically empty. They sat facing each other in an empty compartment. Martha had brought a pile of American magazines. Bannerjee plunged into them and paid little attention to Martha's enthusiastic prattle about the lessons, students who had made passes at her, Paris and her folks back home. They got to their destination without getting any closer to each other. That *place* of the Seine was crammed with bathers.

Martha became the centre of attraction. Her two-piece swimsuit showed her figure to advantage. Her body seemed to be made of whipcord. And she had the grace and power of Artemis. A group of young men threw a rubber football to her. She hurled it back at them like a discus thrower. It sailed over the heads of the young men and fell several feet beyond them. Martha swam, went on a ski-board and sunbathed on the sand. Bannerjee sat in the canvas chair turning the pages of American magazines.

The train back to Paris was crowded with returning holidaymakers. They were lucky to find places next to each other. Within a few minutes people were standing in the corridors and the aisles. The compartment was full of laughter and the acrid smoke of Gaulloise cigarettes. Martha's hand stole over Bannerjee's knee. She twined her fingers in his.

Many people got off at suburban stations. One station before Gare d'Orleans, Martha and Bannerjee were left to themselves still holding hands. Bannerjee was deeply absorbed in the landscape of sooty houses and railway sidings. Martha released her hand, slipped it round Bannerjee's neck and gently kissed him on the ear. Bannerjee put down the magazine he was pretending to read and turned to Martha. She took him in her arms and pressed her thick lips on his. She kissed him on his eyes, cheeks and ears. She bit him passionately on his neck leaving a dark, lipstick-stained tooth mark. Bannerjee surrendered himself to the onslaught. He felt the girl's hot breath all over his face and neck and smelt the wanton negroid smell of her body. The train slowed down. Martha released Bannerjee from her grasp. She took a wad of paper handkerchiefs from her bag. 'Here, Gulloo darling, wipe your face; I've made such a mess of it.' While Bannerjee scrubbed his lips, chin and eyelids, Martha repainted her lips and daubed her cheeks with rouge. The train pulled up at Gare d'Orleans.

They had a snack at a students' cafe. Martha stretched her arms and stifled a yawn. 'I am tired! All this bathing and the sun and everything else. I must go home. I can fix you a drink in my room to speed you on your way.'

Bannerjee knew what was coming. Could he cope with her?

It was a small room with a bed, an arm-chair and a table. On the table was a silver-framed photograph of Martha's family: her parents, two brothers and two sisters—all large and bony and very Black. On the floor were heaps of different kinds of American magazines. Clothes were strewn on the bed.

Martha poured out two Cinzanos and handed one to Bannerjee. 'Gulloo, here's to us', she said raising her glass—and kissed him on the lips.

'Here's to us, Martha,' replied Bannerjee—and let her kiss him again.

Martha drained her glass in a gulp and placed both her hands on Bannerjee's shoulders. 'Gulloo, I am going to miss you,' she said looking him straight in the eyes.

'Me too,' replied Bannerjee with some effort.

His eyes dropped to her bosom. 'What are you staring at?' she reprimanded without taking her arms off his shoulders. Bannerjee paid his first faltering compliment. 'You know what Martha, you remind me of the picture of Venus. Know the one I mean? By the Italian—of Venus rising out of the sea?'

'Botticelli's *Birth of Venus*? Why, it's the nicest compliment anyone has ever paid me. That calls for another drink.' She refilled the glasses and gave him a gentle kiss on the forehead. Then she stretched herself on her bed with her hands beneath her head. Bannerjee's eyes wandered restlessly on Martha's body.

'And now what are you gaping at, may I ask? One would think you'd never seen a woman before in your life.'

Bannerjee cleared his throat. 'Well,

nothing like this one.'

They fell silent. Martha swallowed what remained in her glass. 'If you promise not to touch me, I will let you see me. I have a nice figure.'

'I promise.'

Martha got up and switched off the light. Bannerjee heard the rustle of clothes and the snap of elastic. 'You can switch on the light now.'

Bannerjee rose from his chair. His eyes remained glued to the nude dimly visible in the glow of the street lamp; his trembling hands caressed the wall. He found the metal knob and pressed it. The light flooded back into the room. He was hypnotized by Martha's large bosom and very black and oversized nipples. With difficulty he forced himself to look lower—to the fuzz of her pubic hair and the broad flanks of her muscular thighs.

'Do you like me?' She clasped her hands above her head and slowly pirouetted round on her toes like a ballet dancer. 'How's that?'

Bannerjee gulped the spittle that had collected in his mouth. 'Beautiful,' he mumbled. He reclined with his back to the wall.

'Come and kiss me.' Martha held out her arms to him. Bannerjee advanced with uncertain tread and took Martha in his arms. She had made him promise that he would not touch her; and now . . . He kissed her passionately on her breast, her flat belly and navel. Martha grabbed him by his hair and turned his face towards her. 'Patience,' she commanded. Her legs twined about his and she hungrily took his mouth in her own. Passion welled up in Bannerjee's frame and drained out of his system. He went limp in Martha's embrace. Her breath and the odour of her body began to smell unpleasant to him.

'What's the matter, honey?' asked Martha stepping back.

'This is too much for me. I must go home.'

'All right, if that's what you wish.' She wrapped her dressing gown around her and lit a cigarette. There was a scowl on her face.

'No, no, Martha, it is not like that,' he protested. 'It's best, if you don't wish to . . . you know.'

'I suppose so.'

They sat in silence. Bannerjee took her hand. It was cold and unresponsive. She stubbed out her cigarette. 'I am tired, honey,' she said getting up. 'Thank you for the nice day.' She kissed him coldly on the forehead and almost pushed him out. He heard her lock her door behind him.

Three days later, he saw her off on the boat train at Gare St Lazare.

That was thirty years ago.

For many years the vision of Martha standing stark naked in the centre of the room had acted like an aphrodisiac. Although he had failed her and was often mortified by the memory, he invoked her assistance to meet his wife's demands. And more often than not, it was Martha Stack and not Manorama Bannerjee who received the bounty of his ultimate passion. The tropics and the tedium of an eight-hour day, six days a week played havoc with his constitution. However, as the years rolled by, even the figure of the chocolate nude with its oversized, black protruding nipples and fuzzy pubic hair failed to arouse him. He tried to recall when he had last been cajoled to make love to his wife— months, if not a year—and what a job it had been!

'Don't worry honey, we all get old.' That's

what Martha had said.

He did not see a Black woman in the lounge of the Ashoka and rang up Martha's room. 'I'll be down in a second. We've just come back from sightseeing and I thought I'd change for dinner. Won't be long,' she replied.

He watched the elevators come down, disgorge groups of American tourists and shoot up for more. At long last came one with only one passenger; it could not take any more. Filling the entire cage was the form of Martha Stack; six feet tall and broader than any woman Bannerjee had ever seen. She waddled out and held out her fat, fleshy arms to greet him. 'Honey, you've gone fat,' she exclaimed pointing to his little paunch. Bannerjee held out a limp hand. 'Martha, I can't say you haven't changed.'

Martha put her arms on her ample waist. 'Now that's not a very nice thing to say to an old friend, is it?' She roared with masculine laughter. 'I've put on a bit of weight, haven't I? I am going to shake it off before I get home. Let me drop my room key.'

She wheezed up to the hall porter's desk. The metamorphosis staggered Bannerjee. Her behind was one enormous mass of hulking

flesh; her waist had assumed the same
proportions as her bosom and her posterior.
Even her neck which had been so slender
had accumulated fat. And her once athletic
legs were stumpy, like those of English
charwomen. She was like the picture of Aunt
Jemima advertising good, wholesome, instant
pudding.

Martha took Bannerjee's arm to walk
down the carpeted stairs. Bannerjee noticed
the sniggers of the bellboys; the
commissionaire turned away and exchanged a
lewd remark with the nightwatchman.
Martha's voice was as loud as her dress. She
heaved herself into the front seat of
Bannerjee's tiny Fiat Millicento. 'Not meant
for an oversized American,' she exclaimed
heartily.

At home Martha fared better than
Bannerjee had expected. Her unabashed
compliment—'Why you old so-and-so, where
did you pick up such a lovely wife?'—made
her doubly welcome. She handed out gifts:
her own lipstick to Bannerjee's daughter, a
ballpoint pen to the son, a compact to
Mrs Bannerjee. Mrs Bannerjee was kind and
condescending; even if her husband had ever

desired Martha, there was nothing physically
desirable about her now. The evening passed
well.

Martha glanced at her watch. 'I've got to
get up early to catch my plane; I think I
should be getting back. Can I get a cab?'

'My husband will drop you at the hotel,'
insisted Mrs Bannerjee. 'Wish you could have
stayed longer.' Bannerjee knew that if it had
been an attractive woman, his wife would
have 'volunteered' to keep him company, or
asked one of her children to accompany him
to 'take a little fresh air'.

Martha kissed Mrs Bannerjee and her
children and again squeezed herself into the
Fiat Millicento. 'Nice family you have,' she
said. 'That wife of yours is certainly pretty.
Must have been quite a smasher in her time.'

'She retains her youth better than I,'
answered Bannerjee, 'some people are made
that way.'

He boldly took her arm up the stairs and
to the hall porter's desk. Martha looked at her
watch again. 'If you'd like a quick drink, I can
fix you one in my room. I can make up for
lost sleep in the plane tomorrow.'

'For old times' sake,' replied Bannerjee

stepping into the elevator. After the dismissal of Martha as a woman by his family, he felt it was up to him to make it up to her.

Martha got two tumblers from the bathroom and fetched a bottle of Scotch from her wardrobe. She held it up against the light. It was almost half full. 'Must finish it, no point taking whisky back with you. Soda or water?'

'A splash of soda for me, please.' Bannerjee got up to take his drink. They clinked glasses; Bannerjee gave her a gentle kiss on the lips.

'This seems pretty familiar to me except for the follow up. Too fat for that sort of thing!' she said smiling broadly. Her gums showed like red rubber. 'Thank you honey, this has made my journey worthwhile. I was wondering if you'd ever kiss me again.'

She poured out another drink, sank into an armchair and waived Bannerjee to the sofa, 'Do sit down.' The gesture was clearly meant to keep Bannerjee at a distance. Bannerjee noticed the gold necklace with a cross dangling between her bosom; perhaps she had become religious—or like him, just old and indifferent to sex. Bannerjee sipped

his Scotch; he could hardly bare to look Martha
straight in the face. And yet he did not want
to do anything which would betray his
disappointment, and hurt her. He poured
himself a third drink and came and sat on the
arm of Martha's chair. He put his hand on
Martha's forehead. Her skin was greasy. He
tried to run his fingers through her hair; it was
like tangled wire gauze. He looked down at
her. She had shut her eyes and seemed quite
unconcerned. Bannerjee turned up her face
and pressed his lips on hers. She sat
impassively without opening her mouth.
Bannerjee realized that the poor thing had
lost all confidence. He slid off the arm of the
chair and into her lap and kissed her more
tenderly.

Visions of the Martha he had known in
Paris came back to him and a forgotten passion
warmed his limbs. Both of them slid off the
chair down onto the floor. Martha lay back—
an enormous mound of flesh without any
animation. Her eyes remained closed—as
though she could not bear to look at herself.
Bannerjee's hands went searching for her
undergarments. She protested weakly, 'What
will your wife have to say!' Bannerjee knew
he could not let her down this time.

Bindo

Dalip Singh lay on his charpoy staring at the star-studded sky. It was hot and still. He was naked save for his loincloth. Even so, beads of perspiration rolled off from all parts of his body. The heat rose from the mud walls which had been baking in the sun all day. He had sprinkled water on the roof of the house, but that only produced a clammy vapour smelling of earth and cow dung. He had drunk as much water as his stomach would hold, still his throat was parched. Then there were the mosquitoes and their monotonous droning. Some came too close to his ears and were caught and mashed between his palm and fingers. One or two got into his ears and he rammed them against the greasy walls with his index finger. Some got entangled in his beard and were squashed to silence in their snares. Some managed to gorge themselves on his blood, leaving him to scratch and curse.

Across the narrow alley separating his house from his uncle's, Dalip Singh could see a row of charpoys on the roof. At one end slept his uncle, Banta Singh, with his arms and legs parted as if crucified. His belly rose and fell as he snored. He had had bhaang in the afternoon and slept with utter abandon. At the other end of the row, several women sat fanning themselves and talking softly.

Dalip Singh lay awake staring at the sky. For him there was no peace, no sleep. Yet, on the other roof slept his uncle, his father's brother and murderer. His womenfolk found time to sit and gossip into the late hours of the night while his own mother scrubbed the pots and pans with ash and gathered cow dung for fuel. Banta Singh had servants to look after his cattle and plough his land while he drank bhaang and slept. His black-eyed daughter Bindo went about doing nothing but showing off her Japanese silks. But for Dalip Singh, it was work and more work.

The keekar trees stirred. A soft, cool breeze blew across the rooftops. It drove the mosquitoes away and dried the sweat. It made Dalip feel cool and placid, and he was heavy with sleep. On Banta Singh's roof, the women stopped fanning themselves. Bindo stood up beside her charpoy, threw her head back and filled her lungs with the cool fresh air. Dalip watched her stroll up and down. She could see the people of the village sleeping on the roofs and in the courtyards. No one stirred. Bindo stopped and stood beside her charpoy. She picked up her shirt from the two corners which fell just above her knees and held it across her face with both hands, baring herself from the waist to her neck, letting the cool breeze envelop her flat belly and her youthful bust. Then someone said something in an angry whisper, and Bindo let down her shirt. She dropped down onto her charpoy and was lost in the confused outlines of her pillow.

Dalip Singh was wide awake and his heart beat wildly. The loathsome figure of Banta Singh vanished from his mind. He shut his eyes and tried to recreate Bindo as he saw her in the starlight. He desired her, and in his dreams, he possessed her. In his dreams, Bindo was always willing—even begging. Dalip, condescending—even indifferent; Banta Singh, spited and humbled. Dalip Singh's eyes were shut but they opened into another world where Bindo lived and loved, naked, unashamed and beautiful.

Several hours later, Dalip's mother came and shook him by the shoulder. It was time to

go out ploughing while it was cool. The sky
was black and the stars brighter. He picked
up his shirt which lay folded under his pillow
and put it on. He looked across to the
adjoining roof. Bindo lay fast asleep.

Dalip Singh yoked his bullocks to the
plough and let them lead him to the fields.
He went through the dark, deserted lanes of
the village to the starlit fields. He was tired,
and the image of Bindo still confused his
mind.

The eastern horizon turned grey. From
the mango grove the koel's piercing cries
issued in a series of loud outbursts. The
crows began to caw softly in the keekar trees.

Dalip Singh was ploughing but his mind
was not in it. He just held the plough and
walked slowly behind. The furrows were
neither straight nor deep. The morning light
made him feel ashamed. He decided to pull
himself together and shake off his day-
dreaming. He dug the sharp point of his
plough deep into the earth and thrust his
goading stick violently into the hind parts of
the bullocks. The beasts were jerked into
movement, snorting and lashing their tails.
The plough tore through the earth and large

clods of earth fell on either side under Dalip's
feet. Dalip felt master of his bullocks and the
plough. He pressed the plough deeper with
savage determination and watched its steel
point concupiscently nosing its way through
the rich brown earth.

The sun came up very bright and hot.
Dalip gave up the ploughing and led his
bullocks to a well under the peepul tree and
unyoked them. He drew several buckets of
water. He bathed himself and splashed water
over his bullocks, and followed them home
dripping all the way.

His mother was waiting for him. She
brought him freshly-baked bread and spinach,
with a little butter on it. She also brought a
large copper cup full of buttermilk. Dalip fell
on the food eagerly, while his mother sat by
him fanning away the flies. He finished the
bread and spinach and washed it down with
buttermilk. He laid himself on a charpoy and
was soon fast asleep. His mother still sat by
him fanning him tenderly.

Dalip slept right through the morning
and afternoon. He got up in the evening and
went round to his fields to clear the water
courses. He walked along the water channel

which separated his land from his uncle's. Banta Singh's fields were being irrigated by his tenants. Since he had killed his brother, Banta Singh never came to his land in the evening.

Dalip Singh busied himself clearing the water channels in his fields. When he had finished doing that, he came to the water course and washed himself. He sat down on the grassy bank with his feet in the running water and waited for his mother.

The sun went down across a vast stretch of flat land, and the evening star shone close to a crescent moon. From the village he could hear the shouts of women at the well, of children at play—all mixed up with the barking of dogs and the bedlam of sparrows noisily settling down for the night. Batches of women came out into the fields and scattered behind the bushes to relieve themselves. They assembled again and washed in rows along the water course.

Dalip Singh's mother came with the wooden token from the canal timekeeper that indicated that Dalip's turn to water his field had started. Then she went back to look after the cattle. Banta Singh's tenants had already left. Dalip Singh blocked the water exit to Banta Singh's land and cut it open to his fields. After doing this he stretched himself on the cool grassy bank and watched the water rippling over the ploughed earth, shimmering like quicksilver under the light of the new moon. He lay on his back looking at the sky and listening to the noises from the village. He could hear women talking somewhere in Banta Singh's fields. Then the world relapsed into a moonlit silence.

Dalip Singh's thoughts were disturbed by the sound of splashing water close to him. He turned around and saw a woman on the opposite bank sitting on her haunches washing herself. With one hand she splashed the water between her thighs, with the other she cleaned herself. She scraped a handful of mud from the ground, rubbed it on her hands and dipped them in the running water. She rinsed her mouth and threw handfuls of water over her face. Then she stood up leaving her baggy trousers lying at her feet. She picked up her shirt from the front and bent down to wipe her face with it.

It was Bindo. Dalip Singh was possessed with a maddening desire. He jumped across

the water course and ran towards her. The
girl had her face buried in her shirt. Before
she could turn around, Dalip Singh's arms
closed round her under the armpits and across
her breasts. As she turned around, he
smothered her face with passionate kisses and
stifled her frightened cry by gluing his mouth
to hers. He bore her down on the soft grass.
Bindo fought like a wildcat. She caught Dalip's
beard in both her hands and savagely dug her
nails into his cheeks. She bit his nose till it
bled. But she was soon exhausted. She gave
up the struggle and lay perfectly still. Her
eyes were shut and tears trickled down on
either side, washing the black antimony on to
her ears. She looked beautiful in the pale
moonlight. Dalip was full of remorse. He had
never intended hurting her. He caressed her
forehead with his large rough hands and let
his fingers run through her hair. He bent
down and tenderly rubbed his nose against
hers. Bindo opened her large black eyes and
stared at him blankly. There was no hate in
them, nor any love. It was just a blank stare.
Dalip Singh kissed her eyes and nose gently.
Bindo just looked at him with a vacant
expression, and more tears welled in her eyes.

Bindo's companions were shouting for her. She did not answer. One of them came nearer and shouted for help. Dalip Singh got up quickly and jumped aross the water course and was lost in the darkness.

II

The entire male population of the village of Singhpura turned up to hear the case of Crown v Dalip Singh. The court room, the veranda and the courtyard were packed with villagers. At one end of the veranda was Dalip Singh in handcuffs, between two policemen. His mother sat fanning him with her face covered in a shawl. She was weeping and blowing her nose. At the other end, Bindo, her mother and several other women were huddled together in a circle. Bindo also wept and blew her nose. Towering above this group were Banta Singh and his friends leaning on their bamboo poles, in constant and whispered consultation. Other villagers whiled away their time buying sweets from hawkers, or having their ears cleaned by itinerant 'ear specialists'. Some were gathered round vendors of aphrodisiacs nudging each other and laughing.

Banta Singh had hired a lawyer to help

the government prosecutor. The lawyer collected the prosecution witnesses in a corner and made them go over their evidence. He warned them of the questions likely to be put to them by the defence counsel. He introduced the court orderly and the clerk to Banta Singh and made him tip them. He got a wad of notes from his client to pay the government prosecutor. The machinery of justice was fully oiled. Dalip Singh had no counsel nor defence witnesses.

The orderly opened the courtroom door and called the case in a sing-song manner. He let in Banta Singh and his friends. Dalip Singh was marched in by the policemen but the orderly kept his mother out. She had not paid him. When order was restored in the courtroom, the clerk proceeded with reading the charge.

Dalip Singh pleaded not guilty. Mr Kumar, the magistrate, asked the prosecuting sub-inspector to produce Bindo. Bindo shuffled into the witness box with her face still covered in her shawl and blowing her nose. The inspector asked her about her father's enmity with Dalip Singh. He produced her clothes stained with blood and semen.

That closed the case for the prosecution. The evidence of Bindo corroborated by the exhibits was clear and irrefutable.

The prisoner was asked if he had any questions to put forward. Dalip Singh folded his handcuffed hands.

'I am innocent, possessor of pearls.'

Mr Kumar was impatient.

'Have you heard the evidence? If you have no questions for the girl, I will pass orders.'

'Thou of the pearls, I have no lawyer. I have no friends in the village to give evidence for me. I am poor. Show mercy. I am innocent.'

The magistrate was angry. He turned to the clerk. 'Cross-examination—nil.'

'But,' spluttered Dalip Singh, 'before you send me to jail, emperor, ask her if she was not willing. I went to her because she wanted me. I am innocent.'

Mr Kumar turned to the clerk again.

'Cross-examination by accused: Did you go to the accused of your own free will? Answer . . .'

Mr Kumar addressed Bindo: 'Answer, did you go to the accused of your own free will?'

Bindo blew her nose and wept. The

magistrate and the crowd waited in an impatient and irritated silence.

'Did you or did you not? Answer. I have other work to do.'

Through the many folds of the shawl muffling her face Bindo answered.

'Yes.'

Jean Memsahib

John Dyson dismounted on the summit of the hill and surveyed the scene. The red brick rest house was situated in the centre of a small clearing in the jungle. On all sides where the hill sloped down was a high wall of trees with creepers climbing from the trunks and spreading out like cobwebs among the branches. The only opening was on the side from which the road led down to the valley. One could see a densely wooded valley stretching away for several miles.

The baggage had already arrived and lay piled in the veranda. Near the servants' quarters, the coolies were sitting on their haunches smoking by turns, a small clay hookah. The overseer sat on a steel chair talking to them.

The hookah party at the servants' quarters broke up, and the overseer walked over to meet Dyson.

'Lovely garden,' said Dyson, addressing the overseer. 'Who's been looking after it?'

'There is an old mali, sahib. He's been living here some fifty years—as long as the house has been here.'

A skinny old man pushed his way through the crowd and bowed to Dyson with folded hands. '*Gareeb purwar* (defender of the poor), I am the mali. I have been a mali ever since I was fifteen. Jean Memsahib brought me here and now I am sixty. Jean Memsahib died here. I too will die here.'

'Jean Memsahib? Would that be Cotton's wife?' asked Dyson, turning to the overseer.

'No, Sir, no one knows much about her. She was a social worker—or a teacher—or a missionary or something. She built this bungalow and had a school for children. Then she died suddenly and no one seems to know anything about her. The Government took over the building and converted it into a forest officers' rest house.'

The conversation was interrupted by the shouts of coolies coming up with the palanquin chairs carrying Mrs Dyson and her daughter Jennifer.

'Old mission school' said Dyson, waving towards the house. 'Not a bad spot, is it?'

The family surveyed the scene in silence. The setting sun lit the house, the lawns, the flower beds and the teak forest with its creepers, in a haze of golden light. It was quiet and peaceful. The distant murmur of the stream in the valley emphasized the stillness of the evening.

The coolies and the overseer left for the village in the valley before sunset. The Dysons got busy settling in. The bearers went about lighting hurricane lanterns, laying the dinner table, and fixing mosquito nets on the beds. Mrs Dyson and Jennifer went round inspecting the rooms. Dyson stretched himself on a large cane armchair in the veranda, lit his pipe and ordered a Scotch. He watched the setting sun fire the monsoon clouds in a blaze of burnished gold, then a copper red, orange, pink, white, and finally a sulky grey. The tropical jungle was hushed into an eerie stillness as the twilight sank into night. The birds settled down, and within a few minutes it was quite dark. Now the jungle was alive with a different variety of noises, the croaking of frogs and the calls of jackals and hyenas. As Dyson sat sipping his Scotch and smoking, the fireflies came out on the lawn almost up to where he was sitting.

The bearer announced dinner. The dining table was lit with candles. From the mantelpiece a hurricane lantern spread a sickly yellow light on the grey plaster walls discoloured by age and monsoon rains.

There was very little talk at the dinner table. Only the bearer coming in or going out with plates and courses, and the tinkle of crockery and cutlery broke the oppressive silence. Jennifer was fidgety. She had been exploring the house when the bearer had interrupted her with summons to the dining room. Suddenly she put down her knife and fork with a loud clatter—

'Look, mummy, there's a picture on the wall.'

Mrs Dyson shuddered and turned back to look. The distemper on the wall was discoloured by long lines where rain water had trickled down from the ceiling to the floor. There were many patterns on the wall which changed shape with the flickering of the lamp.

'Jennifer,' said Mrs Dyson hoarsely, 'do stop frightening me and get on with your dinner.'

The rest of the meal was eaten in silence. Jennifer was sent to bed when the coffee was brought in.

Mrs Dyson looked back at the wall once more. There was nothing on it.

'John, I don't like this place.'

Dyson lit his pipe with deliberation, pressing down the tobacco with a match box.

'John, I don't like this place,' repeated Mrs Dyson.

'You are tired. You'd better get to bed.'

Mrs Dyson went to bed. Her husband joined her after a while, and in a few minutes he was asleep and snoring.

Mrs Dyson could not sleep. She propped her pillows against the poles of the mosquito net and stared at the garden. It was a moonless night but the sky was clear and the lawn was dimly starlit. Beyond the lawn was the forest, like a high black wall. The frogs and the insects, an occasional screech of a bird, the laugh of a hyena and the howling of jackals filled the jungle with noises. This brought cold sweat on Mrs Dyson's forehead.

Many hours later, a pale moon came up over the crest of the jungle and lit the garden with a sickly glow. The dew covered the lawn in a gossamer white.

Mrs Dyson decided to take a walk to shake off the feeling of eeriness. The grass

was cool and wet under her bare feet. As she
walked she looked at the green trail she left
in the dewy whitewash on the grass. She
shook her head as if throwing off a weight,
and took several deep breaths. It was fresh
and exhilarating. There was nothing eerie
and nothing to be frightened of.

Mrs Dyson strolled up and down the
moonlit lawn for several minutes. Feeling
refreshed, she decided to go back to bed. Just
as she approached the veranda, she stopped
suddenly. A few paces ahead of her, the lawn
showed footprints. A trail continued to be
marked by invisible feet till the edge of the
clearing and then disappeared into the jungle.
Margaret Dyson felt feverish and weak in the
knees and collapsed.

When she recovered, it was nearly
morning. The whole countryside was alive
with the singing of birds. Mrs Dyson dragged
herself to bed utterly exhausted.

When the bearer brought in the tea, the
sun was streaming across the veranda. Dyson
had had his breakfast and was ready to go out.
At the further end of the lawn, the overseer
and coolies were waiting for him.

Dyson was back shortly before sunset.

He ordered his whisky and soda and stretched out his legs for the bearer to unlace his boots. With a couple of whiskies in him, he became jovial.

'What are we having for dinner? Smells like curried chicken. I am hungry—can't beat the country air!'

The family had their dinner in silence, Dyson enjoying the food. A jackal walked up the lawn almost to the dining room door and set up a howl. Mrs Dyson's fork fell from her hands. Before her husband could speak, she stood up and said in a hoarse whisper: 'John, I don't like this place.'

'Your nerves are in a bad way. It was only a jackal. I'll shoot a few. They won't disturb you. There's no need to be jittery. Did you sleep well last night?'

'Yes, thank you.'

'I saw you walking on the lawn, Mummy,' butted in Jennifer.

'You eat your pudding and go to bed,' answered Mrs Dyson.

'But I saw you, Mummy—you were in your white dressing gown and you looked inside my net to see if I was asleep and I shut my eyes. I saw you.'

Mrs Dyson went pale.

'Don't talk nonsense, Jennifer, and go to bed. I haven't got a white dressing gown and you know it.' Mrs Dyson got up from the table and her husband joined her.

'Did you have a disturbed night?'

'I couldn't sleep at all. But, John, I haven't got a white dressing gown and I did not look into Jennifer's bed.'

'Oh, this is all hooey. Come on, Jennifer, finish your pudding and off to bed. I'll get my gun and shoot one of these jackals. Would you like a jackal for a fur coat, Jennifer?' said Dyson, affecting a hearty manner.

'No, I don't like jackals.'

Dyson got his gun, loaded it, and stood it against the wall near his bed. He lit his pipe and kept up a continuous conversation till it was time to go to bed.

'If you hear any jackals,' he said to his wife, 'just wake me up.'

'Yes, dear.'

Within a few minutes, Dyson was fast asleep.

Jennifer was also asleep. But Mrs Dyson lay in bed with her eyes wide open staring through the net at the lawn and the wall of trees that was the jungle.

Out of the misty haze emerged a figure of a woman in a long white dressing gown. Her hair was tied in two plaits which fell on her shoulders. Her features were not discernible but her eyes had an inhuman brightness. Mrs Dyson turned cold, petrified with fear. She tried to scream, but only a muffled moan escaped her. John Dyson continued to snore.

The phantom figure started moving towards the veranda, fixing Mrs Dyson with a stare. When it was halfway across the lawn, a jackal scampered across and stood facing it. The animal raised its head and sent up a long howl, and immediately, others joined in the chorus.

Mrs Dyson found her voice and her moan changed into a frantic shriek.

John Dyson got up with a start and darted for his gun. Before he could collect his wits and take aim, the jackals dashed away in different directions. Dyson emptied both his barrels at one of them, but was well out of range.

'Missed the bastard' Dyson muttered to himself.

Next morning, the Dysons' nerves were more frayed than ever.

'I am sorry, dear, I frightened you last night,' said Dyson, 'I must get those jackals tonight.'

'John, didn't you see anything else?'

'Else, what else?'

'A woman in white. She was walking straight at us when you fired the gun.'

'Nonsense. I am sorry I missed the jackal. You must pull yourself together.'

'But, John, you must believe me. The first night I saw her footprints on the lawn.'

Mrs Dyson paused, and then got up. 'Come and see.'

She led her husband to the lawn, still milky white and shimmering in the sunlight. There were the footprints. Dyson followed them till he came to a clearing. In the centre of the clearing was a grave—an old dilapidated grave without any stone or inscription. The moss had grown all over it and from the cracks in the plaster grew weeds and ferns.

Dyson was shaken but did not change his tone. 'This is too damned silly for words,' he said.

When the overseer arrived. Dyson sent

for him in his office and shut the door behind him.

'Sunder Lal, what do you know about this house?'

'Not much, sir,' faltered the overseer. 'Many stories are told in the villages around here and superstitious folk believe them. The house has remained unoccupied for many years, and even after the Government acquired it, Indian officers refused to stay here. But the mali has been here all this time and seems quite happy.'

'Send for the mali.'

Sunder Lal fetched the mali.

'The Sahib wants to know about the house. Tell Sahib all you know.'

'Defender of the poor,' said the old mali speaking in Hindustani, 'the house was built by Jean Memsahib who came from Mandla. She had a school for children. It was on government land, and after many years of litigation, the Government won and acquired it.'

'What happened to Jean Memsahib?' asked Dyson.

'She died in this house, Sahib. After the Government acquired the house she closed her school. Then she fell ill. She used to walk about in the garden during the rainy season and got malaria. She died after many attacks. Only Riaz, her Muslim bearer, and I were present. We went down to Mandla to inform the Sahibs there, but no one seemed to know about her. We buried her in the forest. Riaz left and is now in Mandla working as a bearer. I stayed on with the Government.'

'How many people lived in this house after her death?'

'No one has lived here, Sahib. Officers come and go. People have spread tales about her having cursed the place. But I have lived here more than fifty years and no harm has come to me.'

Dyson dismissed the overseer and the mali and went to his wife.

'Just had a word with the mali and the overseer' announced Dyson nonchalantly, 'lot of poppycock about no one being able to stay in this house. The mali's been here for fifty years. In any case, I am going to stay right here and settle this ghost once and for all.'

That night, Dyson again loaded his gun and removed the safety catch. After dinner he drank several cups of black coffee. He had a hurricane lamp put beside his bed, and he began to look at some old copies of *Blackwood's Magazine* he had found in an almirah. Comforted by the light and the knowledge of her husband being awake, Mrs Dyson fell fast asleep as soon as she put her head on the pillow.

For some time, Dyson smoked his pipe and read. Then he dimmed the lantern and just smoked.

The night was darker than the two previous ones. It was clouded over and a damp breeze indicated rain. Some time well after midnight, there was lightning and thunder and it began to rain in torrents, as it does in the tropics. The breeze carried a thin cooling spray across the veranda and into the mosquito nets. Mrs Dyson and her daughter slept through the lightning and thunder. The cool spray made Dyson sleepy. He began to nod and then dozed off sitting against his pillow.

A jackal came up close to the veranda and sent up a howl. Dyson woke up with a jerk. Just then the lamp flickered and went out. Through the net Dyson saw the outlines of a human figure standing at the foot of his bed. A pair of bright eyes fixed him with a steady stare. There was a flash of lightning and he saw her—the woman in white with plaits falling about her shoulders. The thunder which followed the lightning shook him into activity. With a cry of fear he leapt out of bed and groped for his gun, not taking his eyes off the figure beside his bed. He caught the butt and wildly went for the trigger. There were two loud reports. Dyson fell with the full discharge of the gun in his face.

Dhanno

There were still another four days to Sunday, when most papers carried matrimonial ads. And it would be another week or ten days before anyone would respond. Nevertheless, Mohan looked more carefully at the advertisement pages to see if any carried mid-week matrimonials. None did.

As he sat down for his post-breakfast Havana (Romeo and Julieta—Rs 150 each), the sweeper woman came in carrying her broom, a bucket of phenyl water and a mop and asked him if she could do the floors. She had taken orders from his wife about which room to do first: their bedroom, the children's room and the bathrooms were given priority; the sitting-dining room came last. Without looking up at her, Mohan nodded his head.

As she sat on her haunches mopping the floor with a piece of rag soaked in phenyl, Mohan noticed her rounded buttocks separated by a sharp cleavage. He could not take his eyes off her ample behind. He had never bothered to look at her before nor did he know her name. She was just the

jamadarni—sweeper woman. She often
brought her three children with her. He had
sometimes seen them playing in the garden
while their mother was busy in the house.
The sweeperess stood up, turned her face
towards him and brushed aside a strand of
hair from her forehead. He noticed that she
was full-bosomed and had a narrow waist. She
was dark but not unattractive. The woman
got down on her haunches again to do another
part of the room. Mohan turned to his paper.

He recalled his college days in India.
One of the boys had told him that sweeper
women made the best lovers; they were
uninhibited, wild and hot. Mohan had often
reflected that as a class, the so-called
untouchable women were in fact the most
touchable. What about this one in his own
house? It would not be very difficult to
persuade her to come to his bedroom when
the other servants were in their quarters or
out buying provisions. He could double her
salary, give her children toys and sweets.
Such master-servant liaisons were not
uncommon. Poorly-paid menials welcomed a
second income and their spouses were not
very particular about infidelity provided it

brought in some money. No messy hassles with women demanding attention and presents and wanting to be taken out to parties. There was also the advantage of convenience: sex on the tap, as it were. Mohan decided to keep the sweeper woman in mind in the event of failure on other fronts. She would provide no companionship but would at least solve his most important and most immediate problem: his need for sex.

Sarojini

Professor Sarojini Bharadwaj arrived at the house a couple of hours after Mohan had left. Jiwan Ram and the bearer took her cases to the guest room.

After the servants had left, she looked around the room. Her eyes fell on an envelope on the pillow. She tore it open. She felt the thick wad of currency notes. For a moment she felt ashamed of herself, then put the money in her handbag. She read the note. It said nothing about the money. He had fulfilled his part of the contract in advance; he was a gentleman, true to his word. She had no option but to fulfil her part of the deal.

Sarojini unpacked, arranged her clothes in the empty wardrobes and laid out her books on the work table. By the time she had finished her bath, it was 10 a.m. She had toast and a cup of coffee for breakfast, then told the bearer that she was going out to do some shopping and would be back in time for lunch.

Sarojini was not familiar with New Delhi's shopping areas but had heard that the best saris were to be found at the South Extension market. The chauffeur knew exactly where to take her. They made slow progress on the Ring Road choked with overcrowded buses and more cars and two-wheelers than she had ever seen. At the Moolchand traffic light, a fancy steel-grey car stopped next to their Mercedes. Sarojini found herself examining the woman in the back seat. She had her hair permed, her lips painted a bright red, and rouge on her cheeks. She wore a sleeveless blouse with a plunging neckline. There was a prosperous looking man sitting next to her, with gold rings on his fingers. The man put his arm around her, pulled her to him and said something in her ear. The woman threw her head back and laughed, a manicured hand at her cleavage. 'Slut,' hissed Sarojini under her breath. It was only after the lights had changed and the cars were moving that Sarojini realized what she had done. She had condemned a woman who perhaps was doing nothing worse than what she herself had agreed to do. Only, she, Sarojini Bharadwaj, Professor of English, did not look the type. For the second time that morning, she felt ashamed of herself. But the feeling soon died.

Only a vague apprehension remained.

The market was crowded, but the chauffeur took her to a shop where it did not take her long to find what she wanted. She bought herself a beige-coloured cotton sari— beige suited her best—and a pink dressing gown. The two cost her a little over a thousand rupees. While paying for them, she counted the notes. The purchases and what remained amounted to exactly ten thousand rupees.

She was back in time for lunch. The bearer had laid out an elaborate meal of cucumber soup, vegetable pilaf, daal and vegetable curry, followed by rice pudding. She sampled everything but ate very little. She locked herself in her room and tried to get some sleep.

But sleep would not come to her. Her mind was agitated. She dozed off for a few minutes, and woke up to check the time. Dozed off again, then woke up with a start and again looked at her watch. It seemed as if time had come to a stop. She switched on her bedside lamp and tried to read, but her mind was too disturbed to take in anything. She gave up, closed her eyes and resumed her battle with sleep. So passed the restless afternoon. She heard the servants return from their quarters. By the time she came out to have tea it was 5 p.m. She found herself looking at her wristwatch every few minutes. As it came closer to 6 p.m., the time when Mohan left the office, her nervousness increased. She went back to her room and had yet another bath—her third of the day. She lit sticks of agar and put them in a tumbler that she placed in front of a figurine of Saraswati, her patron goddesss, that she always carried with her. She sat down on the carpet, joined the palms of her hands in prayer and chanted an invocation to Saraswati. Her prayers told, she changed into the beige sari she had bought that morning, put a fresh bindi on her forehead, a light dab of colour on her lips and splashed cologne on her neck and breasts. She put on her pearl necklace and examined herself in the bathroom mirror. Still nervous, she went out and sat in the balcony to await Mohan's arrival.

The days had begun to shorten; daylight faded away sooner than in the summer months. By half-past six the brief twilight had given way to the dark. The evening star twinkled in the darkening sky beside a half moon. Not

long afterwards Sarojini heard the car drive
up to the gate. The driver got out of the car,
opened the iron gate and drove in the sleek
black Mercedes with its lights dimmed. Saroj
heard Mohan respond to the driver's 'Good
night, sir' in English. She heard him come up
the stairs. 'What's the smell?' he asked loudly.
'Hello,' said he as he walked out to the
balcony and took the chair next to hers.
'Everything okay? Lunch, tea, bedroom?'

'Hello,' she replied, standing up.
'Everything's fine. That's the aroma of the
agar I lit for Saraswati. I do Saraswati puja
every evening. Do you mind the smell?'

'Not at all; just not used to it. Please sit
down. So what did you do all day?'

'A little shopping. I bought this sari,
thanks to you.' She held up the hem of the
sari to show him.

'Very nice. And what else?'

'Unpacked, arranged my clothes and
books, had lunch, read a little, slept a little,
and the day was gone.'

They had nothing more to say to each
other. Mohan got up. 'If you'll excuse me for
a few minutes, I'll take a quick shower and
change. The office is a very sweaty place.

Too many hands to shake. Too many dirty files to read.' He loosened his collar and took off his tie.

The first thing he did was to turn on his answering machine. It had recorded no incoming calls. He shaved himself, took a shower and splashed on some aftershave. He got into a sports shirt and slacks and joined Sarojini on the balcony. The bearer brought out his Scotch, soda and a bucket of ice cubes. 'Have you never had a drink?' he asked.

'You mean alcohol? My husband-for-a-month made me try whisky. I didn't like the taste and spat it out. Then he gave me some kind of sweet wine which I did not mind. It didn't do anything to me.'

'It must have been sherry. I have some very good Spanish Oloroso, a ladies' drink. You'll like it.'

He got up and pulled out a wine glass and the Oloroso from his drinks cabinet. He poured out the sherry for her and a stiff Scotch for himself.

'This is not bad at all,' she said, taking a sip. 'I hope it won't make me drunk.'

'A couple of glasses will do you no harm.

There's hardly any alcohol in it,' he replied.

Their conversation became stilted: 'So, tell me some more.' 'No, you tell me more about yourself. I have done nothing really interesting today.' And so on.

Sarojini kept pace with Mohan's drinking and felt she was floating in air. Mohan felt she was drinking to fortify herself against what was to come. They had dinner (vegetarian for both) without exchanging many words. The servants cleared the table, had their meal in the kitchen and left for their quarters. Mohan got up to lock the doors. Sarojini saw him chain and lock the front gate and then disappear into the house to lock the servants' entrance. He came out into the front garden, faced a hedge and unbuttoned his flies. She heard the splash of his jet of urine on the leaves. 'Curious fellow!' she said to herself. She went into her bedroom, took off her sari, petticoat and blouse, and slipped on the new silk dressing gown. She was a little unsteady on her feet and slumped down in her chair. Mohan latched the rear door and came up to join her. He took her hand in his and asked, 'Are you okay?'

'Yes. Only a little tired. I should not have

drunk all that sherry. I'm not used to alcohol. I'll sleep it off,' she said standing up.

'Let me see you to your bedroom,' he said putting his arm round her shoulder and directing her towards her bed. She put her head against his broad chest and murmured, 'Be gentle with me. I have not been near a man for eleven years. I'm scared.'

He took her in a gentle bear hug to reassure her. 'There's nothing to be scared of; I'm not a sex maniac. If you don't want it, we won't do it. Just let me lie with you for a while and I'll go back to my room.'

Sarojini felt reassured but clung to him. Mohan laid her on the bed and stretched himself beside her. She dug her face in his chest, clasped him by the waist and lay still. He slipped his hand under her dressing gown and gently rubbed her shoulders and the back of her neck. Then her spine and her little buttocks. The tension went out of her body and she faced him. 'Switch off the table lamp,' she said.

'You don't want me to see your body?' he asked as he switched off the lamp.

'There is not much to see,' she replied. 'I'm like any other woman of my age. Only plainer. And not as well endowed.'

'Let's have a dekho,' he said as he undid
the belt of her gown and cupped one of her
breasts in his hand. Indeed, she was not as
well endowed as his wife or Dhanno or any of
the other women he had bedded. The
difference made her more desirable. He kissed
her nipples and took one breast in his mouth.
She began to gurgle with pleasure. 'Don't
neglect the other one,' she murmured. He
did the same to the other breast. He
unbuttoned his trousers and she felt his stiff
penis throb against her belly.

'My God you are big!' she exclaimed in
alarm. 'This thing will tear me to pieces.' She
clasped it between her thighs to prevent it
from piercing her. 'Promise you won't hurt
me. Remember I'm very small and have had
no sex for a very, very long time.'

He felt elated, macho and grandly
overpowering. And he was more patient than
he had been with other women. He sensed
she was ready to receive him. She spread out
her thighs and he entered her very slowly.
'Oh God, you will split me into two,' she said
clasping him by the neck. She was fully
aroused. In a hoarse voice she whispered

urgently, 'Ram it in.' He did as he was told.

She screamed, not in agony but in the ecstasy of a multiple orgasm. She had never experienced it before nor believed it was possible. Her body quivered, and then relaxed . . . Then all of a sudden, a fit of hysteria overtook her. She clawed Mohan's face and arms and chest and began to sob. 'I'm a whore, a common tart! I'm a bitch,' she cried. Mohan held her closer and reassured her, 'You are none of those; you are a nice gentle woman who has not known love.'

She knew his words meant nothing but they were strangely soothing. She rested her head on his arm and was soon snoring softly. Neither of them felt the need to wash and fell asleep in each other's arms. Many hours later it was Sarojini who shook Mohan awake. 'Better go to your own room and make your bed look as if it has been slept in.'

Mohan staggered out of her room. He did not know what time it was. He undid the latch of the servants' entrance and lay down on his bed. He was fast asleep within minutes.

Yasmeen

I met Yasmeen while attending classes in comparative religion in the department of religion and philosophy.

I had begun to enjoy the lectures on religion by Dr Ashby, our professor. There was a motley group of students in his class from different disciplines—medicine, literature, engineering and others. Among the thirty-odd who were regulars, there were two nuns, and a woman in salwar-kameez in her late thirties. She wore a lot of gold jewellery and was heavily made-up. Since she did not wear a bindi, I presumed she was a Muslim. She sat in the front row. I was always a back-bencher. After each lecture, there were discussions, and some students, the Muslim woman in the front row in particular, had much to say. I took no part in them since I knew very little about any religion.

Dr Ashby took us through the world's major religions: Zoroastrianism, Jainism, Buddhism, Judaism, Hinduism, Christianity and Islam. I was most interested in hearing what he had to say about Hinduism. Despite being a Hindu, I knew almost nothing about my religion besides the names of Hindu gods and goddesses and the Gayatri mantra. Three lectures were devoted to Hinduism. Dr Ashby told us of the four Vedas, the Upanishads and the Bhagvad Gita. They made more sense to me than the other religious texts he had dealt with. 'Worship God in any form you like, that, essentially, is what Hinduism says,' explained Dr Ashby. 'Hindus have no prescribed scriptures: no Zend-Avesta, no Torah, no Bible, no Koran. Read what moves you the most. Seek the Truth within yourself.' And how spiritually elevating the message of the Gita was—*Nish kama karma*: do your duty without expectation of reward. When you engage in the battle of life, do so regardless of whether you win or lose, whether it gives you pleasure or pain. There was also the Lord's promise to come again and again to redeem the world from sin and evil-doing. Hinduism had no prophets, no one God, we were told. One could choose any deity one liked and worship him or her. By the end of that lecture I felt elated and wanted to shout: 'I am a Hindu and proud of being one.'

It was that woman in the front row who

dampened my spirits. She launched into a
furious monologue. 'Professor,' she began as
soon as Dr Ashby had finished, 'what you said
about Hindu philosophy is all very well. But
tell us, why do the Hindus of today worship
a monkey as a god, an elephant as a god; they
worship trees, snakes, and rivers. They even
worship the lingam, which is the phallus, and
the yoni, the female genital, as god and
goddess,' she screeched, thumping her desk.
'They have obscene sculptures on their temple
walls. They have deities for measles, smallpox
and plague. Their most popular god, Krishna,
started out as a thief and lied when caught
thieving; he stole girls' clothes while they
were bathing so he could watch them naked;
he had over one thousand mistresses; his
lifelong companion was not his wife but his
aunt Radha. Hinduism is the only religion in
the world which declares a section of its
followers outcastes by accident of birth.
Hindus are the only people in the world who
worship living humans as godmen and
godwomen. I am told that there are nearly
five hundred such men and women who claim
to be bhagwans. They believe a dip in the
Ganges washes away all their sins, so they can

start sinning again! What basis is there for their belief that after death you are reborn in another form depending on your actions in this life? You may be reborn as a rat, mouse, cat, dog or a snake. *This* is what the Hindus of today believe in, not in the elevated teachings of the Vedas, Upanishads and the Gita! Should we not examine these aspects of Hinduism as practised today?'

There was stunned silence. The woman had spoken with such vehemence that there was little room left for objective dialogue. Dr Ashby restored the atmosphere to an academic level. 'This sort of thing could be said about all religions,' he said gently. 'What their founders taught and what their scriptures stand for are far removed from how they are interpreted and practised today. Our concern is with theory, not practice. Muslims condemn the worship of idols, yet they kiss the meteorite stone in the Kaaba and millions worship the graves of their saints.'

'I can explain Muslim practices,' replied the lady.

Before she could do so, however, the class was over.

'We will resume this discussion next

week,' said Professor Ashby as he left the classroom.

I was fuming with rage. As the class began to disperse, I quickly walked up to the woman and asked her, 'Madam, why do you hate Hindus so much?'

She was taken aback. 'I don't hate Hindus,' she protested. 'I don't hate anyone.' She looked me up and down as if she was seeing me for the first time. It had not occurred to her that I could be an Indian. She was contrite! 'Are you a Hindu from Bharat?' she asked.

'I am,' I replied as tersely as I could, 'and proud of being both. And I don't worship monkeys, elephants, snakes, phalluses or yonis. My religion is enshrined in one word, ahimsa— non-violence.'

She apologized. 'Please forgive me if I hurt your feelings. Perhaps one day you will enlighten me and clear the misgivings I have about Hindus and Bharat.' She put out her hand in a gesture of friendship. I shook it without much enthusiasm.

'My name is Yasmeen Wanchoo,' she said. 'I am from Azad Kashmir on a leadership grant.'

'I'm Mohan Kumar, from Delhi. I'm in business management and computer sciences.'

Like many Kashmiri women, Yasmeen was as fair-skinned as Caucasian women. She had nut-brown hair, large gazelle eyes and was fighting a losing battle with fat. She had a double chin, her arms had sagging flesh and there were tyres developing about her waist. She was, as the Punjabis say, *goree chittee gole matole*—fair, white and roly-poly. She was the first Pakistani woman I had ever spoken to, also the first Muslim. I wanted to know if there was any truth in the stories I had heard about Pakistanis hating Indians and the contempt Muslims had for Hindus. I hoped Yasmeen Wanchoo would tell me. It was not very long ago that our two countries had fought a war—their third—but I did not hate Pakistanis. Her outburst had shocked me. I have never understood hatred.

At the next class, she came up to me and said, 'No hard feelings. Come and sit next to me.' I declined. 'Madam, I sit in the last row, I hate being in the front.'

'In that case I'll sit with you in the last row. And do not "Madam" me, it makes me feel old. I am Yasmeen. And if you don't mind I'll call you Mohan.'

At the time, I had no steady date so I kept company with Yasmeen. She turned out to be not as aggressive as I had thought, and I began pulling her leg often about her being anti-Hindu and anti-Indian. She told me more about herself. 'My parents lived in Srinagar, now the capital of India-occupied Kashmir. Our forefathers were Brahmin Pandits till they had the good sense to convert to Islam. It is the best religion in the world. My parents lived in Srinagar till the Indian army occupied it, then they migrated to Muzaffarabad, the capital of Free Kashmir. I was born and educated there. I married another refugee from India, a Kashmiri, also of Brahmin descent—though Muslims, we don't marry below our caste. My husband is a minister in the Azad Kashmir Government. I am also active in politics and a member of the Assembly. We have three children.' I asked her if she did not prefer the freedom she had in America to her life in Pakistan. She would not give me a straight answer. When I persisted, she got a little irritated and said, 'I love my family and my *watan*. We may not have succeeded yet; but one day we will liberate Kashmir from India's clutches and I will return to Srinagar which I have only seen in pictures.'

'And plant the Pakistani flag on Delhi's Red Fort,' I quipped.

'Inshallah!' she replied, beaming a smile at me.

'One day we will liberate your so-called Azad Kashmir from the clutches of Pakistan and make it a part of Indian Kashmir again.'

'You live in a fool's paradise,' she said warming up. 'One Muslim warrior can take on ten of you Hindus.'

'So it was proved in the last war,' I replied sarcastically. 'The Pakistani army laid down arms after only thirteen days of fighting. Ninety-four thousand five hundred valiant Muslim warriors surrendered tamely to infidel Hindus and Sikhs without putting up a fight. In the history of the world there is no other instance of such abject surrender of an entire army.'

'Now you are being cruel,' she said, almost whining. 'You Indians are cheats. You misled those miserable Bengalis to rise against their Muslim brethren. Now they hate your guts and want to regain our friendship. You see what happens in the next Indo-Pak war.'

Despite our heated arguments, Yasmeen and I became friends. She could hardly be described as my date as she was almost twenty years older than me. She sought my company because there were not many men or women of her age on the campus. Though young, I was at least from her part of the world; she could talk to me in Hindustani. We often had coffee together. One day, out of the blue, she gave me a Gold Cross pen as a gift. I did not have much money to spare as I sent much of what I saved from my stipend along with what I earned doing odd jobs in the library or working in the cafeteria, to my father. However, I started looking into shop windows to find something suitable as a return gift for Yasmeen.

After a couple of weeks, Professor Ashby went on to Islam. He gave us a long list of books to read—various histories of the Arabs, biographies of Prophet Mohammed, translations of the Koran, essays on Muslim sects and sub-sects. I did not bother to read any of them. What I looked forward to was Yasmeen's comments after the lectures. She did not disappoint me.

She kept her peace during the first two lectures in which Professor Ashby dealt with pre-Muslim Arabia, the life of the Prophet, revelations of the Koran, the Prophet's flight from Mecca to Medina, his victorious return to Mecca, the traditions ascribed to him, the speed at which his message spread to neighbouring countries, the Shia-Sunni schism and so on. It was factual information but not very inspiring. As soon as he had finished his second lecture, Yasmeen shot up from her seat beside me and delivered an impassioned harangue. 'What you have told us about Islam is historically accurate, Dr Ashby. What you haven't told us is why it is today the most vibrant of religions. This is because it is the most perfect of all religious systems with precise rules of dos and don'ts that everyone can follow. It was only to Prophet Mohammed (peace be upon Him) that God Himself sent down His message for mankind. Mohammed (peace be upon Him) was the most perfect human being that ever trod the face of the earth. There must be some reason behind the spectacular success of His mission. Within a few years of His death, Islam spread like wildfire from the Pacific Coast to the Atlantic

Coast of Europe; it spread all over Asia and the African continent. It overcame the opposition of fire worshippers, Jews, Christians, Buddhists and Hindus. Why does Islam gain more converts than any other religion? These are some of the questions that I would like the class to discuss.'

She sat down breathless after her speech. Only one student, a mild-mannered Jew who always wore a skullcap, took up her challenge. 'Perhaps the lady can answer some of my questions before I answer hers,' he said. 'Can she deny that Islam borrowed most of its ideas from Judaism? Their greeting, *salam valaikum*, is derived from the Hebrew *shalom alech*; the names of their five daily prayers are taken from Judaism. We turn to Jerusalem to pray; they borrowed the idea from us, but instead, turn to Mecca. Following the Jewish practice, they circumcise their male children. They have taken the concept of *haraam* (unlawful) and *halaal* (legitimate), what to eat and what not to eat, from the Jewish kosher. We Jews forbid eating pig's meat because we regard it unclean; Muslims do the same. We bleed animals to death before we eat them. Following us, so do they. They revere all the prophets revered by Jews and Christians. What was there in Islam which was very new? Everything it has is borrowed from Judaism or Christianity.'

Yasmeen was up on her feet again to do battle with the Jew. 'What was new was the advent of Prophet Mohammed (peace be upon Him). He was the greatest of all prophets sent by Allah. That is why we call Him the seal of Prophets—Khatm-un-Nabi. We recognize no one after Mohammed (peace be upon Him).'

The Jew did not take that lying down. 'What about the division between Sunnis and Shias? Shias pay greater deference to the Prophet's cousin and son-in-law Ali, than they do to the Prophet. And what about Muslim sects founded on sub-prophets of their own? The Aga Khans, Ismailies, Bohras, Ahmediyas and many others whose names I can't even remember? And while we are at it, I would like the lady to enlighten us on why, when Islam talks of giving a fair deal to women, it allows four wives to one man, why many Muslim rulers maintained large harems of women and eunuchs. Why are they forever calling for jehad—holy war—with infidels and fighting against each other?'

It was degenerating into a pointless wrangle. Professor Ashby put an end to it. 'I see we are in for another lively debate. Perhaps you can discuss these issues outside the class.'

The lecture period was over. Yasmeen's face was flushed with anger and triumph. 'Don't you think I put that miserable Jew in his place?' she asked me as we walked out. Instead of answering her question, I asked her, 'Yasmeen, why are you so *kattar* (bigoted)? Muslims are the most bigoted religious community in the world. Their Prophet was the greatest, their religion is the best, Muslims are the most enlightened community, the most God-fearing and righteous of all mankind. If the Jews think they are God's chosen people, Muslims think they are the choicest of the chosen. How can you be so narrow-minded?'

She was taken aback. 'We are not bigoted,' she retorted. 'We follow our religious precepts in letter and in spirit because we know they are the best for humanity. You must give me the opportunity to tell you of the beauty of Islam. You don't know what you are missing in life.'

'I'm happy in my ignorance,' I replied. 'I don't have much patience with any religion. All I say is try not to injure anyone's feelings. The rest is marginal. Gods, prophets, scriptures, rituals, pilgrimages mean very little to me.'

She made no comment.

*

Yasmeen had only a week left in Princeton. Having failed to find anything more suitable to give her, I bought her a University ring made of silver with the Princeton emblem on it. At a coffee session one morning when no one was sharing our table, I took it out of my pocket and slipped it on her finger. 'I see you wear only gold but I could not afford a gold ring. And this being a University ring, no one will comment on it. You could have bought it yourself but I'm giving it to you so that it will remind you of your days with a Bharatiya Hindu boy in Princeton.'

She took my hand and kissed it.

A faint blush came over her face. 'You are a nice boy. I only wish your name was not Mohan Kumar but Mohammed Kareem, or something like that,' she laughed. 'I am not

as *kattar* as you think. I am just concerned
about your future.'

During her last week in Princeton, we
met every day. We spent the afternoons
walking around the campus and shopping.
She bought lots of things for her husband and
children and her household in Muzaffarabad.
She seemed to have plenty of cash and dollar
traveller's cheques. Came her last day, she
invited me over for dinner. 'Have you ever
tasted Kashmiri food? It is the tastiest in the
world, only very rich. I am a good cook. I can
make very good *goshtaba*. Ever tasted *goshtaba*?'

I admitted that I had not.

'You must tell me what you don't eat,'
she said. 'You Hindus have so many food
fads. I know you don't eat beef or veal, but
believe me, it is the most delicious meat. So
many of you are vegetarian; no fish, not even
eggs. Some even refuse to eat onions or garlic.
How can you make anything tasty without
onions or garlic, I ask you?'

'I eat everything except beef. Not that I
regard the cow as sacred, but because I have
been brought up like that. And let me assure
you that pig's meat, which you will not touch,
can be very clean and tasty: ham, bacon, pork

are the staple diet of most Europeans and
Americans. One reason why I don't think
Islam will spread to the Pacific islands is
because their economy is based on the pig.
And I know that like the Jews, many Muslims
don't eat shrimps, crabs or lobsters. Muslim
tribes living along the Arabian and African
coast don't eat fish because they think fish
are serpents of the sea.'

'You are a very argumentative fellow,'
she said patting my cheek. 'Come as early as
you can tomorrow evening and sample my
Kashmiri cooking. I don't drink, but I'll get
some beer for you and put it in the fridge.'

I swear I had nothing more on my mind
than spending a pleasant evening with
Yasmeen. Things did not turn out that way. I
took her a bunch of dark red roses. She kissed
my hands as I gave them to her and embraced
me warmly. While I was casually dressed in a
sports shirt and slacks, she wore a silk salwar-
kameez with gold borders, a gold necklace
with a medallion on which was inscribed a
verse from the Koran, gold earrings and gold
bangles. She had a lot of make-up on and had
doused herself with French perfume. Besides
beer in the fridge, she had put a half-bottle of

Scotch, a tumbler and a pitcher of water on the centre table. 'You help yourself to Scotch or beer while I say my evening *namaaz*.'

She went to her bedroom, put her prayer mat on the floor and stood facing Mecca. I poured myself a Scotch. While I sipped it, I saw her going through her genuflections. She sat a long time on her knees with the palms of her hands open in front of her face as if reading their lines. I could see her lips moving but could not hear what she was reciting. She looked serene. She turned her face one way, then the other, brushed her face with her hands and stood up. She rolled up her prayer mat and tucked it under her bed.

She went into the kitchen to make sure the *goshtaba* was cooking nicely and lowered the flame so that it could cook slowly. Then she came and joined me. 'How's the drink?' she asked. 'Very nice,' I replied. 'Would you like one?'

'*Toba!* It is *haraam*. You will make me a sinner, will you? You can fetch me a Coke from the fridge.'

I got out a can of Coke. Before I could open it, she took it from my hand and put it on the table. Then she held my hands in hers and looked into my eyes till I had to lower my gaze, embarrassed. Suddenly, she put her arms round my neck and said, 'It is our last evening together. Make love to me—something to remember you by for the rest of my days.'

To say that I was shocked would be an understatement. This was the last thing I had expected of the evening. Besides, Yasmeen had never appeared sexually desirable to me. But she did not give me a chance to protest. She took me by my hand and led me to the bedroom. She took off everything save her jewellery. Her skin was soft but flabby. Her big breasts sagged and she had shaved her pubic hair. None of the girls I had bedded shaved their privates. I was surprised to find that a woman so large who had borne three children, had such a small vagina. It looked vulnerable. While I gazed at her figure, she took off my shirt and pulled down my trousers. She gasped at what she saw. '*Mashallah!* What have you got there? Do all Hindus have organs of this size? It must be their reward for worshipping the phallus.' She fondled it for a while with her pudgy hands, her lips glued to mine.

She pulled me over her and stretched her thighs wide to receive me. I entered her. She moaned with pleasure and locked her legs behind my back. She ate up my face with bites and passionate kisses. We came together.

She lay back exhausted. Then she pushed me off her and went into the bathroom to wash. She came back and put on her kameez. 'That *goshtaba* must be ready by now. It must not get overcooked. You wash yourself and I'll lay the dinner on the table.'

I did as I was told. She was like a political boss in full command of the situation. We sat down to eat. I noticed she had not put on her salwar. Her kameez hung down to her knees, exposing her broad thighs when she stood up or sat down. I understood that she had not finished with me and expected another session after dinner. I was not sure if I would be up to it with her. But I let myself in for it by a thoughtless gesture. While she was washing the dishes and I was drying them with a piece of cloth, I put my right hand under her kameez and stroked her huge buttocks. They were like two gourds of a tanpura joined together—massive, rounded, smooth. She smiled and kissed me on the lips. 'You want to do it a second time? So do I. We will make it different this time.' That did it.

For a while we sat holding hands and chatted away. She told me of her daily schedule in Muzaffarabad. 'With both my husband and I being in politics, we hardly have a moment to ourselves. It is like a public durbar from sunrise to sunset. Wherever we go we are surrounded by men and women with petitions. For me, being here is like being on a holiday. I wish I could extend it but my grant is over and my family will want to know why I am not taking the first flight back to Karachi and home.'

She stood up and stretched her arms above her head and stifled a yawn. 'Time for bed,' she said taking me by the hand and leading me to her bed. She gently pushed me on it. 'This time you relax and I'll do all the work!'

She pulled off my trousers and fondled my limp lingam till it was ready for action. She sat astride my groin, spread her ample frame over me and directed my phallus into her. She was wet and eager and my penis slid in easily. Her breasts smothered my face. She held each in turn and put its nipple in my

mouth, urging me to suck it. She kissed me
hungrily and noisily on my nose, lips and
neck, leaving her saliva on me, while she
heaved and thumped me with her huge
buttocks. 'I haven't had sex for six months. I
am famished,' she said as her movements
became more frenzied. 'Fill me up with all
you have, you miserable kafir,' she screamed.
And with a spectacular shudder and a loud
'ah—ah—ah' she collapsed on me like a
lifeless corpse. She did all the fucking. I was
simply fucked.

'Wouldn't it be nicer if we settled Pak-
India problems this way rather than by abusing
each other and fighting?' she asked after a
while.

'Sure,' I replied. 'And with Pakistan
always on top?'

'Of course! Pakistan must always be on
top.'

I was exhausted, and wanted to get away.
She clung to me and begged, 'Please stay the
night with me. I'll feel very lost if you go
away. I promise I won't bother you any more.'

I agreed to spend the night with her and
see her off at the bus stand the next morning.
I could not resist asking her a few awkward

questions. 'You must tell me how you square your belief in Islamic values with what you and I have been doing.'

She paused a long time, staring at me with her large eyes. 'What I did was sinful,' she admitted.

'A sin punishable with death by stoning or beheading?'

'You are right. But Shariat law requires two Muslim eyewitnesses to an act of adultery. Nobody can prove it against me. You, not being Muslim, don't count in a Shariat court.'

'Is that all that matters to you? Doesn't your conscience bother you?'

'The body has its compulsions which Allah understands. He is Raheem (merciful) and Rahman (compassionate). He will forgive me. On my way back home I will perform an *umra* at Mecca and Medina.'

'*Umra*? What is that?'

'The smaller pilgrimage. Hajj is once a year; *umra*, whenever you can make it. I will pray for forgiveness.'

'And be absolved of all your sins? Like Hindus taking a dip in the Holy Ganga?'

'O shut up!' she shouted angrily. 'Don't spoil my last night with you.'

She put her head on my right arm and nestled against me. 'There is an easier way to my being forgiven. If I converted an infidel to Islam, all my sins would be absolved,' she said.

'Sure! Find another Hindu and convert him to Islam. Not me.' We were soon fast asleep in each other's arms.

Molly Gomes

It was Sunday. No office. I slept longer than usual. I picked up Molly, carried her to her room and tucked her into her own bed. 'Sleep as late as you like. It's Sunday. It will be a late breakfast—early brunch. Take your own time.'

She mumbled something I couldn't make out and turned over and went back to sleep.

I opened the front door, picked up the Sunday papers lying in a heap by the gate and went back to my room. I switched on the electric radiator and got back into bed to read the papers. The bearer brought me tea. In half an hour I had run through the six papers and their colour supplements. There was nothing much to read. I went up to the roof to check the arrangements. The two rexine mattresses were lying next to each other, drenched in dew. I walked around the roof. It was higher than the roofs of the other houses. I could see my neighbours; they could not see me. The rooftops were a forest of TV and dish antennae as far as the eyes could see. While strolling around in the chill morning, it occurred to me that I had missed out on my *surya namaskar* for many days. I stood facing the rising sun and went through all the motions. I felt the better for it.

I bathed, changed into a sports shirt and slacks and put on a thick sweater. Molly emerged from her room after ten, freshly bathed and in one of the salwar-kameez sets she had bought the day before. 'How do I look?' she asked looking down at her long shirt.

'Very nice! I suggest you wrap a shawl around you. This weather can be very treacherous.'

She went back and came out with a hand-knitted woollen scarf that barely covered her front. We sat down in front of the electric radiator. I lit my cigar, she lit her cigarette.

'It promises to be a bright, sunny day. The mattresses are on the roof and I've got a bottle of herbal oil to put on my skin. We can sunbathe all afternoon till the sun goes down.'

'That will be lovely,' she replied.

We had a light brunch of hot Chinese sweet-and-sour soup and ham sandwiches. The servants cleared the table and left for their quarters.

'Come and take a look at the *bandobast*,' I said and led her by the hand up the stairs to the roof. The sun was bright and warm. It had dried the dew on the mattresses. A bottle of herbal oil was warming itself in the sun. Molly walked round the roof to make sure that no one could see us.

'You get into a light dressing gown,' she ordered, suddenly very professional and in command, 'I'll get into my working clothes.'

We waited to let the sun get warmer. When we went up again, it was exactly overhead. There was no breeze. 'Perfect for sunbathing,' pronounced Molly. 'Take off your dressing gown and lie down on your stomach.'

I did as I was ordered. She took off her cotton nightie and tossed it on the ground. She had not a stitch on her except the gold chain around her ankle. She came over and sat on my back—astride—as if riding a horse. I could feel her pubic hair tickle the base of my spine. With both her hands she kneaded my spine from bottom to top, over and over again. She pressed her thumbs hard into my shoulder blades, then twisted them, rinsing out all the tension. She filled her palms with warm herbal oil, smeared it on my back, and repeated the process: up the spinal cord, behind the neck to the base of the skull, round the ears, down to the shoulders and back to the base of the spine. She got up, stepped over me twice and again sat down on my back, this time facing my feet. She put more oil in her palms and went over my buttocks and between them, circling my anus lightly, then to my thighs, legs, ankles, down to every toe. This went on for almost half an hour. It was very soothing and sensuous. Every inch of my body was aching to be ministered to by her loving fingers. She stood above me and ordered, 'Turn around.'

I turned around and lay on my back. I got a worm's eye view of her thighs and what they concealed. She sat down on my stomach. She ran her fingers round my nipples. I had not realized a man's nipples could be as sensitive as a woman's. She poured oil on my chest and with open palms rubbed it into my torso many times. Once again she changed positions; now her buttocks were towards my face. As she stretched forward and back, her pubic hair grazed the line of hair running down from my navel to my groin. She slapped a liberal palmful of oil beneath my testicles and rubbed it into my inner thighs, down to the ankles and the feet. She had to lean forward to massage my feet and I had a splendid view of her anus and pubic fluff. I began to react. My penis sprang to full life and slapped against her thigh as it did so. She slapped it down and away. 'Patience!' she admonished.

The massage went on for an hour. I can't recall ever having experienced anything more pleasurable and sensual—even more than sexual intercourse. She wiped her oily hands against her sides and lay down on her mattress, face down. This time I went over and sat astride her, my balls caressing the small of her back as I moved. Though I had not massaged anyone before, I imitated her. I massaged her body from her neck to her toes, first the rear then the front. I glued my lips to her nipples in turn and slowly entered her. It was heavenly. I stayed inside her a long time, both of us motionless. Then I pulled out and asked her to turn around. She lay on her stomach with her legs wide apart. I positioned myself between her thighs and began to massage her buttocks. Come to think of it, a woman's buttocks excite a man more than any other part of her body—more than her lips or breasts or her pussy. And Molly's were beautifully rounded and firm. I found them irresistible and slowly entered her cunt from the rear. She gave a long sigh of pleasure and let me go further and further into her. We did our best to prolong our bliss. Every time I felt I was coming I pulled out and sat still till the crisis had passed. Then we resumed our search for the ultimate truth of bodily existence: at times she pressed into me from above with my hands squeezing and pressing her buttocks to urge her on; then I on top, with her nails stuck into my posterior. When neither of us could hold out any longer, we went at each other like wild animals, tearing and clawing each other's flesh. The climax was the most prolonged that either of us had experienced in our lives.

No words were spoken. Words were superfluous. We lay on our mattresses and let the sun dry up the oil on our bodies. We had been at it for almost three hours.

After worshipping the sun with our bodies in our own unique way, we went downstairs to cleanse ourselves of the oil on them. I fetched two loofahs and gave her one to run over her limbs after she had soaped herself. There is nothing better than a loofah to scrape oil or dirt off one's body. I felt cleaner than ever before. I got into my woollen dressing gown, switched on the electric radiator and lit a cigar. Molly joined me a few minutes later and lit a cigarette.

'That was heavenly,' I said. 'Don't you think so?'

'Never known anything better in my life,' she replied with a smile. 'But let's not try to repeat it.'

'Why on earth not?'

'This kind of lovemaking in which every part of your body makes love to every part of your partner's is a once-in-a-lifetime experience. Dwell on it in your mind, never try to relive it in action. It will be a great disappointment.'

Nooran

Juggut Singh had been gone from his home about an hour. He had only left when the sound of the night goods train told him that it would now be safe to go. For him, as for the dacoits, the arrival of the train that night was a signal. At the first distant rumble, he slipped quietly off his charpoy and picked up his turban and wrapped it round his head. Then he tiptoed across the courtyard to the haystack and fished out a spear. He tiptoed back to his bed, picked up his shoes, and crept towards the door.

'Where are you going?'

Juggut Singh stopped. It was his mother.

'To the fields,' he said. 'Last night wild pigs did a lot of damage.'

'Pigs!' his mother said. 'Don't try to be clever. Have you forgotten already that you are on probation—that it is forbidden for you to leave the village after sunset? And with a spear! Enemies will see you. They will report you. They will send you back to jail.' Her voice rose to a wail. 'Then who will look after the crops and the cattle?'

'I will be back soon,' Juggut Singh said. 'There is nothing to worry about. Everyone in the village is asleep.'

'No,' his mother said. She wailed again.

'Shut up,' he said. 'It is you who will wake the neighbours. Be quiet and there will be no trouble.'

'Go! Go wherever you want to go. If you want to jump in a well, jump. If you want to hang like your father, go and hang. It is my lot to weep. My kismet,' she added, slapping her forehead, 'it is all written there.'

Juggut Singh opened the door and looked on both sides. There was no one about. He walked along the walls till he got to the end of the lane near the pond. He could see the grey forms of a couple of adjutant storks slowly pacing up and down in the mud looking for frogs. They paused in their search. Juggut Singh stood still against the wall till the storks were reassured, then went off the footpath across the fields towards the river. He crossed the dry sand bed till he got to the stream. He stuck his spear in the ground with the blade pointing upward, then stretched out on the sand. He lay on his back and gazed at the stars. A meteor shot across the Milky Way, trailing a silver path across the blue-black sky. Suddenly, a hand was placed on his eyes.

'Guess who?'

Juggut Singh stretched out his hands over his head and behind him, groping; the girl dodged them. Starting with the hand on his eyes, Juggut Singh felt his way up from the arm to the shoulder and then on to the face. He caressed the girl's cheeks, eyes and nose that his hands knew so well. He tried to play with her lips to induce them to kiss his fingers. The girl opened her mouth and bit him fiercely. Juggut Singh jerked his hand away. With a quick movement he caught the girl's head in both his hands and brought her face over to his. Then he slipped his arms under her waist and hoisted her into the air above him with her arms and legs kicking about like a crab. He turned her about till his arms ached. He brought her down flat upon him limb to limb.

The girl slapped him on the face.

'You put your hands on the person of a strange woman! Have you not mother or sister in your home? Have you no shame? No wonder the police have got you on their register as a bad character. I will also tell the

Inspector Sahib that you are a budmash.

'I am only a budmash with you, Nooro. We should both be locked up in the same cell.'

'You have learned to talk too much. I will have to look for another man.'

Juggut Singh crossed his arms behind the girl's back and crushed her till she could not talk or breathe. Every time she started to speak he tightened his arms round her and her words got stuck in her throat. She gave up and put her exhausted face against his. He laid her beside him with her head nestling in the hollow of his left arm. With his right hand hand he stroked her hair and face.

The goods train engine whistled twice and with a lot of groaning and creaking began to puff its way towards the bridge. The storks flew up from the pond with shrill cries and came towards the river. From the river they flew back to the pond, calling alternately, long after the train had gone over the bridge and its puff-puffs had died into silence.

Juggut Singh's caresses became lustful. His hand strayed from the girl's face to her breasts and her waist. She caught it and put it back on her face. His breathing became slow

and sensuous. His hand wandered again and
brushed against her breasts as if by mistake.
The girl slapped it and put it away. Juggut
Singh stretched his left arm that lay under
the girl's head and caught her reproving hand.
Her other arm was already under him. She
was defenceless.

'No! No! No! Let go of my hand! No! I
will never speak to you again.' She shook her
head violently from side to side, trying to
avoid his hungry mouth.

Juggut Singh slipped his hand inside her
shirt and felt the contours of her unguarded
breasts. They became taut. The nipples
became hard and leathery. His rough hands
gently moved from her breasts to her navel.
The skin on her belly came up in goose flesh.

The girl continued to wriggle and protest.

'No! No! No! Please! May Allah's curse
fall on you. Let go of my hand. I will never
meet you again if you behave like this.'

Juggut Singh's searching hand found one
end of the cord of her trousers. He pulled it
with a jerk.

'No,' cried the girl hoarsely.

A shot rang through the night. The storks
flew up from the pond calling to each other.

Crows started cawing in the *keekar* trees. Juggut Singh paused and looked up into the darkness towards the village. The girl quietly extricated herself from his hold and adjusted her dress. The crows settled back on the trees. The storks flew away across the river. Only the dogs barked.

'It sounded like a gunshot,' she said nervously, trying to keep Juggut Singh from renewing his lovemaking. 'Wasn't it from the village?'

'I don't know. Why are you trying to run away? It is all quiet now.' Juggut Singh pulled her down beside him.

'This is no time for jesting. There is murder in the village. My father will get up and want to know where I have gone. I must get back at once.'

'No, you will not. I won't let you. You can say you were with a girl friend.'

'Don't talk like a stupid peasant. How . . .' Juggut Singh shut her mouth with his. He bore upon her with his enormous weight. Before she could free her arms he ripped open the cord of her trousers once again.

'Let me go. Let me . . .'

She could not struggle against Juggut

Singh's brute force. She did not particularly want to. Her world was narrowed to the rhythmic sound of breathing and the warm smell of dusky skins raised to fever heat. His lips slobbered over her eyes and cheeks. His tongue sought the insides of her ears. In a state of frenzy she dug her nails into his thinly bearded cheeks and bit his nose. The stars above her went into a mad whirl and then came back to their places like a merry-go-round slowly coming to a stop. Life came back to its cooler, lower level. She felt the dead weight of the lifeless man, the sand grits in her hair, the breeze trespassing on her naked limbs, the censorious stare of the myriad of stars. She pushed Juggut Singh away. He lay down beside her.

'That is all you want. And you get it. You are just a peasant. Always wanting to sow your seed. Even if the world were going to hell you would want to do that. Even when guns are being fired in the village. Wouldn't you?' she nagged.

'Nobody is firing any guns. Just your imagination,' answered Juggut Singh wearily, without looking at her.

Faint cries of wailing wafted across to the

riverside. The couple sat up to listen. Two shots rang out in quick succession. The crows flew out of the *keekars*, cawing furiously.

The girl began to cry.

'Something is happening in the village. My father will wake up and know I have gone out. He will kill me.'

Juggut Singh was not listening to her. He did not know what to do. If his absence from the village was discovered, he would be in trouble with the police. That did not bother him as much as the trouble the girl would be in. She might not come again. She was saying so: 'I will never come to see you again. If Allah forgives me this time, I will never do it again.'

'Will you shut up or do I have to smack your face?'

The girl began to sob. She found it hard to believe this was the same man who had been making love to her a moment ago.

'Quiet! There is someone coming,' whispered Juggut Singh, putting his heavy hand over her mouth.

The couple lay still, peering into the dark. Five men carrying guns and spears passed within a few yards of them. They had uncovered their faces and were talking.

'Dakoo! Do you know them?' the girl asked in a whisper.

'Yes,' Juggut said, 'The one with the torch is Malli.' His face went tight. 'That incestuous lover of his sister! I've told him a thousand times this is no time for dacoities. And now he has brought his gang to my village! I will settle this with him.'

The dacoits went up to the river and then downstream towards the ford a couple of miles to the south. A pair of lapwings pierced the still night with startled cries: 'Teet-tittee-tittee-whoot, tee-tee-whoot, tee-tee-whoot, tit-tittee-whoot.'

'Will you report them to the police?'

Juggut Sing sniggered. 'Let us get back before they miss me in the village.'

The pair walked back towards Mano Majra, the man in front, the girl a few paces behind him. They could hear the sound of wailing and the barking of dogs. Women were shouting to each other across the roofs. The whole village seemed to be awake. Juggut Singh stopped near the pond and turned around to speak to the girl.

'Nooro, will you come tomorrow?' he asked, pleading.

'You think of tomorrow and I am bothered about my life. You have your good time even when I am murdered.'

'No one can harm you while I live. No one in Mano Majra can raise his eyebrows at you and get away from Jugga. I am not a budmash for nothing,' said he haughtily. 'You tell me tomorrow what happens or the day after tomorrow when all this—whatever it is—is over. After the goods train?'

'No! No! No!' answered the girl. 'What will I say to my father now? This noise is bound to have woken him.

'Just say you had gone out. Your stomach was upset or something like that. You heard the firing and were hiding till the dacoits had left. Will you come the day after tomorrow then?'

'No,' she repeated, this time a little less emphatically. The excuse might work. Just as well her father was almost blind. He would not see her silk shirt, nor the antimony in her eyes. Nooran walked away into the darkness, swearing she would never come again.

Juggut Singh went up the lane to his house. The door was open. Several villagers were in the courtyard talking to his mother.

He turned around quietly and made his way
back to the river.

*

Before going round to other Muslim homes,
Imam Baksh went to his own hut attached to
the mosque. Nooran was already in bed. An
oil lamp burned in a niche in the wall.

'Nooro, Nooro,' he shouted, shaking her
by the shoulder. 'Get up, Nooro.'

The girl opened her eyes. 'What is the
matter?'

'Get up and pack. We have to go away
tomorrow   morning,'   he   announced
dramatically.

'Go away? Where?'

'I don't know . . . Pakistan!'

The girl sat up with a jerk. 'I will not go
to Pakistan,' she said defiantly.

Imam Baksh pretended he had not heard.
'Put all the clothes in the trunks and the
cooking utensils in a gunny bag. Also take
something for the buffalo. We will have to
take her too.'

'I will not go to Pakistan,' the girl
repeated, fiercely.

'You may not want to go, but they will

throw you out. All Muslims are leaving for the camp tomorrow.'

'Who will throw us out? This is our village. Are the police and the government dead?'

'Don't be silly, girl. Do as you are told. Hundreds of thousands of people are going to Pakistan and as many coming out. Those who stay behind are killed. Hurry up and pack. I have to go and tell the others that they must get ready.'

Imam Baksh left the girl sitting up in bed. Nooran rubbed her face with her hands and stared at the wall. She did not know what to do. She could spend the night out and come back when all the others had gone. But she could not do it alone; and it was raining. Her only chance was Jugga. Malli had been released, maybe Jugga had also come home. She knew that was not true, but the hope persisted and it gave her something to do.

Nooran went out in the rain. She passed many people in the lanes, going about with gunny bags covering their heads and shoulders. The whole village was awake. In most houses she could see the dim flickers of oil lamps. Some were packing; others were helping them to pack. Most just talked with their friends.

The women sat on the floors hugging each other and crying. It was as though there had been a death in every home.

Nooran shook the door of Jugga's house. The chain on the other side rattled but there was no response. In the grey light she noticed the door was bolted from the outside. She undid the iron ring and went in. Jugga's mother was out, probably visiting some Muslim friends. There was no light at all. Nooran sat down on a charpoy. She did not want to face Jugga's mother alone nor did she want to go back home. She hoped something would happen—something that would make Jugga walk in. She sat and waited and hoped.

For an hour Nooran watched the grey shadows of clouds chasing each other. It drizzled and poured and poured and drizzled alternately. She heard the sound of footsteps cautiously picking their way through the muddy lane. They stopped outside the door. Someone shook the door.

'Who is it?' asked an old woman's voice.

Nooran lost her nerve; she did not move.

'Who is it?' demanded the voice angrily. 'Why don't you speak?'

Nooran stood up and mumbled

indistinctly, 'Beybey.'

The old woman stepped in and quickly shut the door behind her.

'Jugga! Jugga, is it you?' she whispered. 'Have they let you off?'

'No, Beybey, it is I—Nooran. Chacha Imam Baksh's daughter,' answered the girl timidly.

'Nooro? What brings you here at this hour?' the old woman asked angrily.

'Has Jugga come back?'

'What have you to do with Jugga?' his mother snapped. 'You have sent him to jail. You have made him a budmash. Does your father know you go visiting strangers' houses at midnight like a tart?'

Nooran began to cry. 'We are going away tomorrow.'

That did not soften the old woman's heart.

'What relation are you to us that you want to come to see us? You can go where you like.'

Nooran played her last card. 'I cannot leave. Jugga has promised to marry me.'

'Get out, you bitch!' the old woman hissed, 'You, a Muslim weaver's daughter,

marry a Sikh peasant! Get out, or I will go
and tell your father and the whole village. Go
to Pakistan! Leave my Jugga alone.'

Nooran felt heavy and lifeless. 'All right,
Beybey, I will go. Don't be angry with me.
When Jugga comes back just tell him I came
to say "Sat Sri Akal".' The girl went down on
her knees, clasped the old woman's legs and
began to sob. 'Beybey, I am going away and
will never come back again. Don't be harsh to
me just when I am leaving.'

Jugga's mother stood stiff, without a trace
of emotion on her face. Inside, she felt a little
weak and soft. 'I will tell Jugga.'

Nooran stopped crying. Her sobs came at
long intervals. She still held on to Jugga's
mother. Her head sank lower and lower till it
touched the old woman's feet.

'Beybey.'

'What have you to say now?' She had a
premonition of what was coming.

'Beybey.'

'Beybey! Beybey! Why don't you say
something?' asked the woman, pushing
Nooran away. 'What is it?'

The girl swallowed the spittle in her
mouth.

'Beybey, I have Jugga's child inside me.
If I go to Pakistan they will kill it when they
know it has a Sikh father.'

The old woman let Nooran's head drop
back on her feet. Nooran clutched them hard
and began to cry again.

'How long have you had it?'

'I have just found out. It is the second
month.'

Jugga's mother helped Nooran up and
the two sat down on the charpoy. Nooran
stopped sobbing.

'I cannot keep you here,' said the old
woman at last. 'I have enough trouble with
the police already. When all this is over and
Jugga comes back, he will go and get you
from wherever you are. Does your father
know?'

'No! If he finds out he will marry me off
to someone or murder me.' She started crying
again.

'Oh, stop this whining,' commanded the
old woman sternly. 'Why didn't you think of
it when you were at the mischief? I have
already told you, Jugga will get you as soon as
he is out.'

Nooran stifled her sobs.

'Beybey, don't let him be too long.'

'He will hurry for his own sake. If he
does not get you he will have to buy a wife
and there is not a pice or trinket left with us.
He will get you if he wants a wife. Have no
fear.'

A vague hope filled Nooran's being. She
felt as if she belonged to the house and the
house to her; the charpoy she sat on, the
buffalo, Jugga's mother, all were hers. She
could come back even if Jugga failed to turn
up. She could tell them she was married. The
thought of her father came like a dark cloud
over her lunar hopes. She would slip away
without telling him. The moon shone again.

'Beybey, if I get the chance I will come
to say "Sat Sri Akal" in the morning. Sat Sri
Akal. I must go and pack now.' Nooran hugged
the old woman passionately. 'Sat Sri Akal,'
she said a little breathlessly again and went
out.

Jugga's mother sat on her charpoy staring
into the dark for several hours.

Beena

'Will any of you have the time to go to the temple today?' Sabhrai asked.

'I have to see the Deputy Commissioner first,' answered her husband. 'On days like these there is always danger of Hindu-Muslim riots; all magistrates have to be on duty. I will go if I have the time.'

'I have to be there,' replied Sher Singh. 'We have organized a meeting outside the temple.'

'Visit the temple before you go to your meeting,' snapped his mother.

'And,' added Buta Singh with indulgent pride, 'don't say anything which may cause trouble. Remember my position. I do not mind your hobnobbing with these Nationalists—as a matter of fact, it is good to keep in with both sides—but one ought to be cautious.'

'Oh no, no,' answered Sher Singh. 'I know what to say and what not to say.'

It was not customary to consult the girls. Beena was expected to go with her mother unless there were good reasons for not doing so. She knew her only chance of getting away was to bring up the subject while her father was still there. 'There are only a few weeks left for my exams. I had promised to go to Sita's house to work with her. We help each other with the preparation.'

'Why can't she come here?' asked Sabhrai. She had been getting more and more difficult about Beena going to Sita's house. Her sharp tone made Buta Singh react adversely. He came to his daughter's rescue.

'Let her go to Sita. There will be nobody in the house today to give her lunch or tea. Sita, I will drop you off at Wazir Chand's house.'

That ended the argument. Buta Singh's word was never questioned. The only one left was Champak. Sabhrai was not very concerned with her daughter-in-law's plans. If she came to the temple, she would not say anything. If she decided to shut herself in her room with her radio at full blast as she often did, she would still say nothing. Nevertheless, Champak felt that the situation demanded some explanation from her. 'I haven't washed my hair for a long time. If it dries in time, I will go in the afternoon—if I can find someone to go with. Otherwise I'll stay at home and put away the Granth after evening prayers.'

Buta Singh looked at his wristwatch. 'I must be going,' he announced with a tone of finality and stood up. 'Get your books and things, Beena.'

*

Wazir Chand's home was very much like Buta Singh's except that it was Hindu instead of Sikh and not so concerned with religion and ritual. As a matter of fact, the only evidence of religion in the house was a large colour print of Krishna whirling a quoit, on the sitting room mantelpiece. Wazir Chand's wife occasionally put a garland of flowers round it and touched the base of its frame as a mark of respect. She did the same to a portrait of Mahatma Gandhi which was kept discreetly away in the bedroom.

The real 'God' in Wazir Chand's home was the son, Madan. He was a tall, handsome boy in his early twenties. Being the only son, he had been married off as soon as he had finished school and had become a father in his second year at college. He had not made much progress in his studies, but had more than compensated for that shortcoming by his achievements in sports. His promotion from one class to another had to be arranged by the college authorities. He was doing his sixth year at the college and had not yet taken the degree which normally took four. But the mantelpiece of every room in the house displayed an assortment of silver trophies that he had won in athletics and other team games. He had been captain of the University cricket eleven for three years and had played for his province against a visiting English side. His performance at this match had made him a legend in the Punjab. There were few days in the year when the sporting columns of the papers did not carry some reference to his activities. This was a matter of great pride to his parents. They gave in to every one of his whims; they practically worshipped him.

The only thing in common between the tall and broad Madan and his slim, small sister, Sita, was their good looks. He was bold and easy with strangers; she, almost tongue-tied and shy. His obsession for games was matched by her aversion to any form of sport. He avoided books; she spent all her time with them. He had barely scraped through the exams he had passed; she had won the highest scholarship for girls in the University. The combination of the athletic prowess of one and the academic distinction of the other and the looks of both had made them the most sought-after couple in the University circles. It was after several months' abject admiration and hanging around her that Beena had succeeded in getting to know Sita.

Beena's anxiety to please Sita made her gushing and enthusiastic about everyone and everything in Wazir Chand's home. She addressed Sita's parents in English as 'Uncle' and 'Auntie'. Madan and his wife she addressed as 'brother' and 'sister' in Punjabi. She spent hours playing with their son and teaching him to call her 'Auntie'. Sita was just Sita; but Beena repeated her name as often as she could in every sentence almost as if she feared losing her if she did not.

Madan had just returned from an early morning practice at the nets when Beena came in. His shirt was drenched in sweat and clung to his body displaying a broad hairy chest. Although it was hot, he carried his white flannel blazer on his shoulder. Its outside pocket bore the insignia of the University

with rows of letters in old Roman embossed
in gold thread beneath. He was playing with
his son who was trying to walk in his father's
cricket boots. The scene was too overpowering
for Beena. She rushed to the child, picked
him up and covered him with kisses.

'Ummm, ummm. Little darling wants to
wear Papa's shoes. Namaste Bhraji.'

'Sat Sri Akal,' replied Madan without
getting up or removing the cigarette from his
lips.

Beena hugged the child and wheeled
him round and round; her pigtails flew in the
air. The child began to whimper. She thrust
him into his father's lap. 'He likes you more
than he likes me. Bhraji, where is Sita and
Lila sister and Auntie and Uncle?'

'Father has gone to see the Deputy
Commissioner. Mother is in the kitchen. Sita
is studying. Lila is in her room; she is not
feeling too well. And yours sincerely is at
your service.' Madan got up and bowed.

Beena ignored his pleasantry. '*Hai!* What's
wrong with Lila sister?' she asked with
exaggerated concern; she frequently used 'hai'
to express it. 'Nothing serious, I hope. I must
go and see her.'

'No, no, it's nothing really; nothing. Just a little out of condition,' answered Madan. 'She is in her room.'

Beena picked up the child once more and hurried to Lila's room. Lila explained that she was not really ill; the feeling of nausea came on only in the mornings. When Beena persisted in her enquiries, Lila patted the back of her hand and said she would understand better when she was married. Beena understood and blushed with embarrassment. She sat with Lila till Sita came to take her away. 'Madan says he can take us to a matinee show this afternoon. We can work for two or three hours and then go with him. Lilaji, you will be all right by the afternoon, won't you?'

'I'd better not go. The stuffy atmosphere of the cinema will make me sick and your brother will get cross with me. You two go with him.'

Beena suffered a twinge of conscience. Studies were considered sacred enough to excuse going to the temple. But in her home the cinema was still associated vaguely with sin. The only time the family went to the pictures was to see the life of some saint or

other or some story with a religious theme.
Regular cinema-goers were contemptuously
described as tamasha-lovers. If her mother
learned that she had spent the afternoon at a
cinema instead of the temple, she would use
it as an excuse to stop her from coming to
Sita's house altogether. 'No, I really could
not. I haven't asked my mother,' said Beena
quickly.

'She would not object if you came with
us. I am sure she would not,' assured Sita.

'And yours sincerely is not going to invite
you every day,' added Madan in his half-
baked stage manner as he came in. 'Besides,
we won't tell anyone. We will go in when the
show has started and you can cover your face
during the intermission.' He drew his hand
across his face to imitate a woman drawing
her veil.

'It's not as bad as that,' answered Beena
laughing. 'If I had asked first, it would have
been better.' Before she could check herself
in her imaginary flight to freedom she heard
herself say: 'Of course I'll go with you but we
must work first.'

During the time that Beena went over
her notes and textbooks in Sita's room she

was bothered by what she would say when she got back. If she said nothing and her parents found out, it would take many months to re-establish her credibility. Perhaps she could mention it casually as something she had been compelled to do. She was seventeen and wasn't going to be bullied by her illiterate mother any more. The pictures could be instructive; maybe this one would have a religious theme and she could persuade her mother to see it too. By the time they left the house, her mind was a muddle of fear and rebellion.

A tonga was sent for the two girls. They took their seats in the rear while Madan rode on his bicycle behind them. He wore a new silk shirt with short sleeves and carried his white flannel blazer on his shoulder; the gold crest and rows of initials glittered in the sun. He kept up a loud conversation with the girls in-between nodding and waving to the many acquaintances he met on the road.

The cinema was crowded. Peasants who had turned up for the Baisakhi festival from neighbouring villages were mulling round the cheaper ticket booths and around the stalls that sold soft drinks. The tonga made its way

through the crowd and drove up to the porch.
Two cinema assistants rushed to take Madan's
bicycle. He was a regular visitor and had
admirers all over the city. Besides, he was the
son of a magistrate; and magistrates,
policemen, their friends and families, had
privileges which went hand in hand with
their power.

The manager of the cinema came out to
welcome them and show them to their seats.
Madan took out his wallet and pulled out a
ten-rupee note. The manager caught his hand
and pressed the note and wallet back into
Madan's pocket. 'No question of money,' he
protested. 'It's on the house.' Madan
whispered in his ear that the other girl was
Buta Singh's daughter. The manager turned
to Beena with an obsequious smile. 'How is
your revered father?' he asked, rubbing his
hands. Beena replied politely that he was
well. 'So glad to hear it. We pray to God he
should always remain well. Do convey my
respects to him. And any time any of your
family wants to come to the cinema, please
ring me up. It will be an honour for us—a
great honour.' Beena promised to convey the
information to her father.

The party was conducted to a box reserved for VIPs and pressed to have something to eat or drink. The manager withdrew after extracting a promise that his hospitality would be accepted during the intermission.

Madan took his seat between the two girls. He lit a cigarette and the box was soon full of cigarette smoke and the smell of eau de cologne with which he had doused himself.

The lights were switched off and the cries of hawkers of betel leaves, sweetmeats and sherbets, and the roar of hundreds of voices died down. First came a series of coloured slides advertising soaps, hair oils, and films that were to follow. The literate members of the audience read their names loudly in chorus. Then the picture started and the few recalcitrant talkers were silenced by abuses hurled loudly across the hall.

Madan stubbed his cigarette on the floor and lit another one. In the light of the flame he saw his sister completely absorbed in the film. He held his cigarette in his left hand and put his right hand lightly on the arm of Beena's chair.

Beena's mind was still uneasy about the

consequences of the escapade. She tried to
drive away unpleasant thoughts by
concentrating on the film and enjoying the
feeling of being with Sita and her brother. He
looked so dashingly handsome in his silk
shirt, flannels, and sports blazer; he smoked
with such compelling nonchalance and exuded
that heavenly, cool, and clean fragrance of
good eau de cologne.

Madan's hand slipped down the arm of
the chair and came in contact with Beena's
elbow. For a moment she held her breath. He
seemed to be engrossed in the film and could
not have realized how far his hand had
travelled. She did not remove her elbow lest
the gesture offend him. It was pleasant to
have him so close. His hand stayed where it
was till the lights came on for the intermission.
He casually smoothed his hair and began
discussing the film with his sister.

The manager reappeared followed by a
relay of bearers carrying trays of soda pop,
ice-cream, and potato chips. He started talking
to Sita. Madan turned to Beena. 'You know,
your brother and I have become great friends.
For so many years we have been in the same
University and it is only now that we have got

to know each other. He is the most popular man in the students' circles.'

'More popular than you, Bhraji? I don't believe it. We have all seen you play cricket; so has everyone in the world, my God!'

'Cricket is nothing,' said Madan with disdain. 'Our brother, Sher, will go far. He is almost certain to be elected President of the Students' Union. He is the best candidate and I am getting all my friends to vote for him.'

'Your name alone should win him the election. Everyone in the city knows you. We were at the match when you scored your century against the English eleven. I . . . everyone . . . was so proud of you. Sixer after sixer. Oh, it was wonderful!'

'It is nothing. You could be a good cricketer if you tried. You have an athletic figure.'

Beena blushed. That was the first time anyone had paid her a compliment, and it was Madan, *the* Madan. 'Oh Bhraji, I am no good. I couldn't see the cricket ball coming towards me at that speed.'

'Yes, you could. With those eyes of yours you could hit anything for six,' said Madan, bending close to her to avoid the manager or his sister overhearing.

'*Hai Bhraji*, you are really terrible. Making fun of a girl like me.'

The conversation was interrupted by the bearers coming to collect the empty glasses and plates. The manager was still rinsing his hands with invisible soap. He took his leave promising to appear again at the end of the show.

As soon as the lights went out, Madan put his hand on the arm of Beena's chair. This time she knew it was not an accident. She could hardly believe that anyone, let alone Madan, would want to make a pass at a plain and simple girl like her. It was unbelievably flattering. But he was married and it was obviously wrong. Beena had no doubt about Madan's intentions as his fingers closed around her elbow. Would he get angry if she withdrew? What would Sita say if she saw? Madan began to caress her arm. Beena did not move. Then his hand brushed against her breast. She shrank away into the farthest corner of her chair. Madan calmly lit another cigarette and took no further notice of her.

When they came out of the cinema, the road as far as one could see was a jostling mass of peasants, tongas, bicycles, and hawkers. Around the ticket booths, men were clustered like bees around a hive. Streams of weary, blinking people poured out from the many exits; newcomers stood around impatiently for their turn to go in.

A tonga was waiting for them in the porch and a cinema attendant had Madan's bicycle ready. The manager was there bowing, smiling, and still rubbing his hands. He bade them farewell after many reminders that they were to consider the cinema as their own. They went through the crowd with the tonga driver shouting at the pedestrians loitering on the road. Madan cycled slowly behind. Whenever the tonga stopped, he put his foot on the ground and then cycled on with a slight push. Throughout the journey he did not talk to or even look up at Beena.

Beena was dropped home first. She said a hurried 'namaste' and disappeared inside the house. Fortunately for her, only Champak was in and she seemed too taken up with the radio programme to bother. Beena went to her room and bolted it from the inside. She flung herself on her bed and lay there in the heat. When it got dark she switched on her table lamp and continued crying on her bed staring blankly at the ceiling.

Champak

Buta Singh's home had made some
concessions to Western notions in the matter
of privacy. There were separate bedrooms for
everyone, with the married couple having a
bathroom of their own. Champak spent as
much time as she could in her own room with
her radio. She was also given to taking a long
time at her bath. On religious holidays,
because everyone went out, she stayed at
home. She could then stroll about the
courtyard in her dressing gown with her hair
loose about her shoulders, and she could also
sing loudly to herself.

On Baisakhi day, Sabhrai had ordered
Mundoo to stay at home to scrub kitchen
utensils and heat the water for Champak's
bath. Champak protested there was no need
for hot water, but her mother-in-law had her
way. 'Hair washes better with hot water,' she
had insisted.

Champak sulked in her room. She
switched on the radio and lay on her bed
reading her favourite film magazine. After
some time, she flung the magazine on the

floor and looked out into the courtyard. Mundoo sat on his haunches scrubbing a big brass pitcher with ash. Beside him, on a smoking hearth, was a large tin canister.

'Oi Mundoo, is the water hot or not?'

The boy patted the canister with his dirty hands. 'No, Bibiji not yet. It will be ready in a few minutes.'

He went down on his hands and knees and blew into the hearth. Smoke and ash whirled round the hearth and into his eyes. He stood up and wiped his tears with the hem of his greasy shirt. All he wore besides the shirt was a red loincloth which only covered his front. His buttocks were bare except for the string that ran between them.

'Bring it into the bathroom when it is ready.'

Champak got up, opened her wardrobe, fished out a shaving set hidden between the pile of saris and went into the bathroom. She did not close either the door behind her or the other one which opened into the courtyard. She was not going to let Mundoo restrict her movements. He was just a servant and a grubby little boy at that. She decided to ignore his presence.

After a few minutes she came back to her bedroom without anything on. She put the shaving set back in its place and stood in front of her full-length dressing-table mirror to inspect the results of the operation and admire the contours of her chocolate-brown body. She loosened her hair and turned around to see how she looked from behind. Her hair fell to the point at which her buttocks rose like softly-rounded watermelons. There were dimples on either side of her rear waist. She turned around once more, inhaled deeply, and lifted her breasts with the palms of her hands and then ran her fingers around her nipples till they became rounded like berries. She clasped her arms above her head and wriggled her hips in the manner of hula dancers. She drew her belly in as much as she could and stroked it with her hand down on either side to knees. She studied her face and figure in all the postures she had seen in photographs of nude models. She found the reflection in the mirror to her satisfaction.

In the courtyard, Mundoo finished washing the kitchen utensils and was on his hands and knees once more blowing into the hearth. He looked like a frog with the wrong end up.

Champak smiled to herself and went back to the bathroom. She shut the door that opened into the courtyard without bolting it, and shouted for the bath water. She turned the tap on full force and began to hum the tune coming over the air.

Mundoo lifted the canister of hot water by the wooden rod which ran through it on the top. It was heavy; he carried it a few steps at a time. When he reached the bathroom door, he put it down to regain strength to take it over the threshold. He gripped the handle with both hands, knocked the door open with his forehead, and carried it in. He put the canister beside the bucket and looked up.

'Why don't you knock or call before you come into the bathroom?'

Champak hid her nakedness with her hands between her knees. Her raven-black hair fell on either side of her neck. Her breasts stared out from between her arms. Mundoo stared stupidly at her without replying and then started to back out of the door.

'What shall I mix the water in? Both the bucket and the canister are full.'

Mundoo turned off the tap, tilted the bucket a little to let some of the water run out, and began to pour the hot water from the canister with a small copper mug. His eyes never rose above Champak's knees, nor left them. Champak remained as she was, hiding her nakedness with her hands, watching the boy's embarrassment.

'In future, knock before you come in. Sometimes I have no clothes on.'

*

'I must tell you what happened today. My God! I nearly died of shame.' Champak always added 'my God' or 'by God' whenever she wanted to emphasize something. She also had the habit of turning the conversation to herself. It was either some compliment paid to her, a pass made at her in the street, or someone looking at her lecherously, and it invariably ended the same way: 'my God' or 'by God', the embarrassment had nearly killed her. Her husband paid little attention to these anecdotes, and that evening he had matters of greater importance on his mind so he barely heard what she had to say.

'You should not have stayed alone in the

house all day; you should have come to the fair. What a turnout at my meeting! First we had a march past of the Student Volunteer Corps. No one has seen such smartness from civilians before. The SVC has come to mean something. Then I addressed the meeting. There was absolute pin-drop silence.' 'Pin-drop silence,' was a favourite among his repertoire of clichés. 'Packed to capacity', 'sacrifice all' and 'eschew all differences' were some of the others that he used frequently.

'*Achha!* Wonderful!' she responded enthusiastically. 'You will become a minister in the Government one day and we will have a flag on the top of our house; we will have an official car and peons in uniform. Then we can dismiss this useless Mundoo of yours. Really you've no idea what he is like!'

'Oh, yes, I have,' interrupted Sher Singh impatiently. 'He is just a poor, underpaid boy. The condition of domestic servants is one of the most pressing problems of urban society. We work them twenty-four hours of the day, underpay, underfeed, and underclothe them. Their living quarters are filthy. They are abused and beaten at will. They are dismissed without notice after a disgraceful search of their belongings. It is scandalous. It must stop. I will stop it.' Sher Singh found it hard to switch from oratory to multitudes to talking to individuals.

'I am sure you will. But this Mundoo . . . really!'

'What's wrong with him? He's no different from other servants. The trouble is we never can see our own faults. Whenever I have problems with people, I put myself in their shoes and see their point of view. It is a very good principle.'

Sher Singh and his wife were too full of themselves to listen to each other's tales. They both abandoned the attempt.

It was hot. The ceiling fan only churned the air inside the room. Other members of the family slept on the roof in the cool of the moonlight. Even Dyer the dog, who never left his master's side when he was at home, refused to be in the room at night. Sher Singh had to suffer because of his wife. He looked at his watch. 'It's after eleven. I didn't realize it was so late. I've had such a tiring day.' He stretched his arms and yawned.

'Your mother hasn't come back from the temple. The procession could not have ended.'

'I don't know about her but I could hear father's snores from the courtyard. And there is a light in Beena's room. She must be studying.'

Sher Singh gave himself a long look in the mirror before taking off his turban and uniform. He went into the bathroom, poured a few mugs of water on his body, and came back dripping to dry himself under the fan. He saw himself in the mirror. His paunch showed no sign of reducing. He pulled it in and thought how much nicer it would be if it always stayed there. He bent down and touched his toes three times and re-examined the effect on his middle. He put on his thin muslin shirt and pyjamas. Before switching off the light, he looked around the room to see if everything was in place. Champak had taken off her kimono and lay stark naked on her belly. She had the pillow between her arms, her legs were stretched apart. Sher Singh knew what this meant. 'My God I feel fagged out,' he said wearily and switched off the light.

Champak stretched out her hand and caught her husband's. 'Now it's dark, I can tell you about this Mundoo of yours. He's not all that innocent, you know!'

'Oh? What did he do?' asked Sher Singh
yawning at the same time.

'Come over and I'll tell you,' she
mumbled, tugging at his hand.

Sher Singh rolled over on to her bed and
let her put her hand on his arm. 'When I
bathe, he keeps peeping through the crevices
of the door.'

'How do you know?'

'I know. And today he burst into the
bathroom on the pretext of bringing in the
hot water. I didn't have a stitch on me. Not
one thing! My God, I nearly died of shame.'

'Why don't you bolt the bathroom door?'

'Never occurred to me; I thought
everyone was out. In any case, he should
have knocked before coming in.'

'I suppose so. He's only a little fellow,'
he said. 'Let's go to sleep.' A minute later he
began to breathe heavily.

Champak's body twitched. She moaned
as if in a nightmare and snuggled closer to her
husband. She caught his hand and took it
lower down her body. Sher Singh knew there
was no way out.

'What have you done?'

'Just to give you a little variety.'

Bhagmati

She sits cross-legged in my armchair turning over the pages of a book. Her left hand is clenched into a fist with a cigarette sticking out of her fingers. She sucks noisily at the cigarette and flicks the ash on my carpet. Her hair is heavily oiled and arranged in serried waves fixed by plastic clips shaped like butterflies. She wears a pink sari of glossy, artificial silk with a dark blue blouse of the same material. A pair of white slippers with ribbon bow ties on their toes lie in front of the chair. Bhagmati is the worst-dressed whore in Delhi.

The light of the table lamp reveals a layer of powder and rouge on her face. It does not lighten the colour of her black skin or hide the spots left by smallpox. The kohl in her eyes has run down and smudged her cheek bones. Her lips are painted crimson. Her teeth are stained with betel leaf. Bhagmati is the plainest-looking whore in Delhi.

'*Ajee!* You are back from *vilayat!*' she exclaims as I enter. And without giving me the chance to say yes, continues, 'What kind

of books do you keep? They have no pictures.'
She waggles her head with every sentence
and gesticulates with her hands in the manner
of hijras. 'No pictures, only black letters like
dead flies.' She changes the subject. 'Did you
ever think of your poor Bhagmati when you
were riding those white mares in London?'
Bhagmati is the coarsest whore in Delhi.

Bhagmati is not a woman like other
women. She's told me something of her past
life; I've discovered the rest myself.

Bhagmati was born in the Victoria Zenana
Hospital near Jamia Masjid. When her father
asked the doctor, 'Is it a boy or a girl?', the
doctor replied, 'I am not sure.' Her parents
already had three boys. So they gave their
fourth child a girl's name, Bhagmati. When a
troupe of hijras came to their home to sing
and dance and said, 'Show us your child. We
want to see if it is a boy or a girl, or one of us,'
her father abused them and drove them away
without giving them any money. The hijras
gave her parents no peace. Whenever they
came to the locality to sing and dance at
births or weddings, they would turn up at
their doorstep and say, 'Show us your last
born. If it is one of us, let us take it away.'

Then Bhagmati's mother had two more children—both girls. Both times her father had taken Bhagmati with him to the hospital and asked the doctor to examine her and say whether she was a boy or a girl. Both times the doctor had looked at her genitals and said 'I am not sure; it is a bit of both.' Bhagmati was then four years old. When the troupe of hijras visited them after the birth of his last child, her father gave them twenty-one rupees and said, 'Now I have three sons and two daughters, you can take this one. It is one of you.'

The troupe of hijras adopted Bhagmati. They taught her to sing, clap her hands and dance in the manner of hijras. When she was thirteen, her voice broke and became like a man's. She began to grow hair on her upper lip, around her chin and on her chest. Her bosom and hips which were bigger than a boy's did not grow as big as those of girls of her age. But she began to menstruate. And although her clitoris became large, the rest of her genitals developed like those of a woman. This time she went to see the doctor herself. He said, 'You can do everything a woman can, but you will have no children.'

There are as many kinds of hijras as there
are kinds of men and women. Some are almost
entirely male, some almost entirely female.
Others have the male and female mixed up in
different proportions—it is difficult to tell
which sex they have more of in their make-
up. The reason why they prefer to wear
women's clothes is because it being a man's
world, every deviation from accepted standards
of masculinity is regarded as unmanly. Women
are more generous.

Bhagmati is a feminine hijra. When she
was fifteen, the leader of the troupe took her
as his wife. He already had two hijra wives,
but such things do not matter to them. Instead
of shunning her as a rival, the wives stitched
Bhagmati's wedding dress and prepared her
for the nuptial bed. They shaved the
superfluous hair on her face and body and
bathed her in rose water. They escorted her
to their husband's room. They had their eyes
and ears glued to the crevices in the door.
Later, they often made love to her. Bhagmati
had smallpox when she was seventeen. 'They
gave me up for dead,' she said. 'They threw
me in a hospital where people were dying
like flies. *Seetla Mai* (Mother Goddess of

smallpox) spared me but left her fingerprints all over my face.'

When men came to expend their lust on hijras—it is surprising how many prefer them to women—Bhagmati got more patrons than anyone else in her troupe. She could give herself as a woman; she could give herself as a boy. She also discovered that some men preferred to be treated as women. Though limited in her resources, she learnt how to give them pleasure too. There were no variations of sex that Bhagmati found unnatural or did not enjoy. Despite being the plainest of hijras, she came to be sought after by the old and young, the potent and impotent, by homosexuals, sadists and masochists.

Bhagmati regards a bed in the same way as an all-in wrestler regards the arena when engaged in a bout. Bhagmati is the all-purpose man-woman sex maniac.

Although Bhagmati is a freelance, she continues to live with her husband and co-wives in Lal Kuan. She puts whatever she earns, in the community kitty. In return, she has a roof over her head and a meal whenever she wants it. When she is ill, they look after her. When she is arrested for soliciting, they furnish bail; when she is sentenced by the magistrate, they pay the fine.

How did I get mixed up with Bhagmati? That's a long story which I will tell you later. How did she come to mean so much to me? I am not sure. As I have said before, I have two passions in my life—my city Delhi and Bhagmati. And they have two things in common: they are lots of fun. And they are sterile.

Georgine

It had been a bad year for me. I didn't have many writing assignments and the articles I sold to Indian papers did not get me enough to maintain the lifestyle I was accustomed to. So I registered myself as a guide with the Tourist Department of the Government of India and left my card at foreign embassies and international organizations. During the tourist season between October and March I made quite a bit in tips in foreign currency which I exchanged for rupees at rates higher than the official. I earned commissions from hotels, curio dealers and astrologers for the custom I brought them. Men left me the remains of their bottle of Scotch. Sometimes middle-aged women invited me to their rooms and gave me presents for the services I rendered them.

It was not very hard work. After I had memorized the names of a few dynasties and emperors and the years when they ruled, all I had to do was to pick up a few anecdotes to spice my stories. At the Qutub Minar I told them of the number of suicides that had

taken place and how no one could jump clear
of the tower and come down in one piece. I
told them of Humayun's father, Babar, going
around his son's sickbed four times, praying
to Allah to transfer his son's illness to him,
and how Humayun had been restored to health
and Babar died a few days later. About the
Red Fort and its palaces, I had picked up a
lot of interesting details: from the time Shah
Jahan had built it, the kings who had sat on
the Peacock Throne and were later blinded
or murdered; the British who had taken it
after the Mutiny of 1857; the trials of INA
officers, down to 15 August 1947 when Lord
Mountbatten had lowered the Union Jack
and Nehru hoisted the Indian tricolour on the
ramparts. Once having done my homework,
there was little more to do than impress the
tourists with my learning.

    After a while I began to enjoy my work.
Although I did not find anyone who would
give me a free round-the-world ticket, I could
boast that the world came to me. Once a
cousin who had found a job as a worker in
England told me of the number of white girls
he had 'killed'. They were English girls
working in the same factory. I told him that I

had 'killed' many more Europeans, Americans, Japanese, Arabs and Africans, sitting where I was in Delhi, without having to pay a counterfeit four-anna coin to anyone. The fellow began to drool at the mouth and scratch his testicles with envy.

The only thing that troubled me was that I never got a chance to make friends with anyone. All the Marys, Janes, Francoises and Mikis darlinged and honeyed me for a day or two and then vanished forever. After a few weeks I could not recall their names or faces. All I could recollect was the way they had behaved when I bestrode them. Some had been as lifeless as the bed on which we lay; some had squirmed and screamed as they climaxed. A few had mouthed obscenities, slapped me on the face and told me to fuck off.

It was different with the American Missy Baba, Georgine. My contact with the US Embassy was a man named Carlyle. I do not know what he did in the embassy except that he looked after what he called 'visiting firemen'. He had tried out other guides. Once he was assured that I 'did no hanky panky' with visitors, he put a lot of custom my way.

Americans were my best customers. Despite
their brash manners, they were more friendly
and generous than other foreigners. I was
particularly careful with Carlyle's 'visiting
firemen'. I was respectful, polite and kept my
distance. I opened car doors for them, did not
angle for tips or look eagerly at their tape
recorders, cameras and ballpoint pens. (I knew
they would leave some memento for me.) I
did not take them to emporia to earn
commissions but helped them with their
shopping at the best and cheapest stores. I
never made passes at Carlyle's introductions
and only obliged those who insisted on my
obliging them.

My Oxbridge accent impressed Americans
more than it did the other nationalities; to
them I was a gentleman guide, a well-to-do
fellow fallen on evil days, which was true.

Carlyle introduced me to Georgine.
Georgine was Mrs Carlyle's niece and had
come to Delhi to spend her Christmas
vacations. 'This is Georgine,' Carlyle said
without mentioning her second name. 'And
this is your guide,' without mentioning mine.
I bowed. She said 'Hi.'

As I said before, she was very young,

gawky, freckled, pimpled, snub-nosed—but also large-bosomed and even larger-assed. She wore a tight-fitting sweater with 'Arizona' printed across her boobs and bum-tight jeans frayed at the ends. I asked her what interested her more, people or monuments. She shrugged her shoulders, stuck out her tongue and replied in a voice full of complaint: 'How should I know? A bit of both, I guess.' She proceeded to take snapshots of the Carlyles, the house, the car—then handed me her mini camera so she could be in the pictures as well. She spoke very fast and dropped the g's at the end of most words: goin', comin', gettin', seein'. She was very animated and spoke with her grey eyes and hands; she interspersed her speech with noises like 'unh', and words like 'shucks' and 'crikey', and was constantly sticking out her red tongue.

'What are we waitin' for?' she demanded turning to me the first day after she had finished the photo session.

I opened the rear door of the car for her. She ignored me and bounced into the front seat beside the chauffeur. I took my place in the rear seat. 'Miss . . .'

'The name is Georgine.'

'Miss Georgine, have you . . .'

'Not Miss Georgine; just plain and simple Georgine, if you don't mind.'

'I was going to ask you if you had read any Indian history. We are going to see . . .'

'That's a stoopid question to ask an American high school girl. Why in the name of Christ should I have read Indian history?' I decided to keep cool. We passed through Delhi Gate into Faiz Bazaar. 'What are all these jillions doin'?' she demanded.

'They are not jillions, they are vegetable-sellers. They . . .'

She turned round as if to make sure I were human. 'You don't know a jillion? It is the highest number—more than millions of millions. Even the dumbest American kid knows that.'

'Oh, I see,' I replied tamely. 'The population of Delhi has more than trebled in these last twenty years. It is over four million now.'

'I don't want to know that!' she snapped.

We went out of Faiz Bazaar. On our left, the Royal Mosque, Jamia Masjid; on our right, massive red walls of the Fort. She ordered the chauffeur to stop and took more snapshots.

We drove up to the entrance of the Red Fort. While I queued up to buy a ticket for her, she took photographs: Chandni Chowk, the tongas, hawkers, beggars, everything. She stopped outside the entrance to take pictures of the guards, looked up at the towering walls and exclaimed 'Yee!'

No sooner had we entered the arcade with its rows of shops aglitter with brass, gold and silver thread embroidery, miniature Taj Mahals and other bric-à-brac, than she stretched her arms wide and exclaimed, 'I want everythin' in this crummy bazaar. How much?' She went from shop to shop picking up things and putting them down with a grunt. But she was canny. She parried every attempt to sell her anything.

A marble-seller would say, 'Yes memsahib, some *marbil-varbil*?' and she would shake her head and reply firmly, 'No thanks.'

We came to the Naqqar Khana gate. I cleared my throat. She pulled out her *Murray's Guide* and said: 'Don't tell me. This is where drums were beaten, right? And that red buildin' in front is the Dear one somethin'-or-the-other where the kingee received common folk, right?'

'Right on the mark. It is the Diwan-i-Am, the Hall of General Audience. You don't need a guide, you know everything.'

'No. I don't,' she snapped. Armed with *Murray's Guide* she instructed me on Emperor Shah Jahan, when he had lived, when he had built the palaces, pointed out the figure of Orpheus behind the throne, the Rang Mahal, the 'Dreamin' Chamber', the octagonal Jasmine tower and the 'Dearonee . . .'

'Diwan-i-Khas.'

'Where kingee sat on the Peacock Throne to receive noblemen. Right?'

'Right.'

'Goodee! That pearly mosque built by the kingee's son who locked up Dad and became King Orangeade.'

'Aurangzeb.'

'Aren't I clever?'

'Very! You could make a handsome living as a professional guide.'

'I could at that! I am thirsty. Can I get a carton of milk or a Coke some place?'

'Coke, yes. Milk, no.'

We returned to the arcade. She drank two bottles of Coke, pressed her belly and belched. 'Sorree! I feel good.'

It usually took me over an hour and a half to take visitors round the Red Fort. Georgine did it in twenty minutes. I picked up a marble Taj Mahal encased in glass and nodded to the shopkeeper. He wagged his head to indicate I could have it for free. 'Miss . . . I mean Georgine, this is for you. With my compliments.'

'Me? What for?' she demanded blushing. She grabbed it from my hands and clasped it to her big bosom. 'It's lovely! Thank you.' She gave me a peck on my nose, 'And that's for you bein' so nice to a horrid girl.'

In the car this time, she took the rear seat beside me. When I asked the chauffeur to take us to the Royal Mosque, she protested: 'Nope. One mornin', one buildin'. Okay?'

'That would take us a whole month to do Delhi.'

'Goodie! You can spend every mornin' with me. Won't you like that?'

We drove through Chandni Chowk, Khari Bawli and Sadar Bazaar. Georgine kept taking snapshots and making unintelligible sounds. Then she suddenly turned round, stared at me and giggled, 'Gawd! You are a funny

lookin' man!' she exclaimed. 'If somebody
had told me last week that I'd be ridin'
around with a darkie with a bandage round
his head and a beard round his chin, I would
have died.' I made no comment. She sensed
my resentment. 'Don't mind me,' she added,
'I am always sayin' such dumb, stoopid things.
What have you got under that bandage
anyway?' I made no reply. She grunted an
'unh' and said no more till we were back in
Carlyle's home. As she got out of the car she
asked, 'Can I pull your beard?' Before I could
raise my hand to protect myself she grabbed
it in her hand and gave it a violent tug. She
threw three ten-rupee notes on the seat,
jumped out with the miniature Taj in her
arms, and with a jerk of her big bottom ran to
the door. 'Bye! See you tomorrow.'

The bloody bitch! I muttered to myself.
What she needs is to be put across the knee,
her jeans ripped off and a few hard smacks on
her large, melon-sized bottom. Followed by
buggery.

At the Coffee House I found myself
telling my cronies about Georgine. I didn't
like my Sikh journalist friend referring to her
as 'another quail (I) had trapped.' Nor the

politician warning me against carnal knowledge of a girl of sixteen. When I came out of the Coffee House, it was late in the afternoon. The *jamun* trees were alive with the screeching of parakeets. I wanted to fill my chest and yell her name so loudly that it would be heard all over Connaught Circus—*Georgeeen*—and the traffic would come to a halt. *Georgeen* and the parakeets would stop screaming. And the only sound to be heard would be *Georgine, Georgine, Georgine*, echoing round and round the Circus.

That evening I told Bhagmati about Georgine. As usual she did not like my being so enthusiastic about anyone other than her. I tried to laugh it off by reminding her that Georgine was forty years younger than me. That did not reassure her. And when I took her with greater gusto than usual, she asked, 'What is the matter with you today?' implying 'You are not taking me but that fat-bottomed sixteen-year-old white girl.' She was right.

I was less exuberant in the morning. However, I spent twenty minutes in my cold, damp bathroom dyeing my beard. By the time I turned up at Carlyle's house, I was apprehensive of the kind of reception I would get.

Georgine was outside soaking in the sun.
She looked more grown up. 'How do you like
my new hairdo?' she asked turning her head
sideways. The hair was bunched on top of her
head and tied in a chignon. It made her neck
look longer and bared her small pink ears.

'Very nice! Makes you look like a lady.'

'I am that. Shucks!'

In the car she asked me if I slept with my
turban on.

I replied: 'If you were a little older, I
would have said "Come and find out for
yourself!"'

Her face flushed. 'You are an ole lech!
You makin' a pass at me or somethin'?'

It was my turn to be embarrassed. 'I said
if you were older, and I meant a lot older. I
must be older than your father.'

'I don't buy that kind of crap!'

I laid on some flattery. White people are
not used to flattery and succumb very easily.
She gave me an opening by taking my hand
and apologizing: 'Don't be mad with me. I
don't mean to be nasty.'

'You are not nasty,' I replied taking a grip
on her hand, 'you are the nicest Missy Baba
I've met.'

'Messy what?' she asked, raising her voice.

'Not messy, Missy. No flattery; it is not often I have someone as pretty to take around.'

'Unh' she growled. 'I am not pretty or good lookin' or anythin' like that.'

But it was clear that my compliment had hit the mark. Her face had gone pink with happiness and after a pause she said, 'You're a nice ole man. Can I call you pop? I don't know your name anyhow.'

Girls are more easy to seduce when they are sixteen than when they are a year or two older. At sixteen they are unsure of themselves and grateful for any reassurance you can give them about their looks or brains—either will do. Georgine, despite her brashness, proved very vulnerable. I took her to the Coffee House, as I said, 'to show her off to my friends.' She blushed again and repeated, 'You *are* an ole lech you know! But I like you.'

At the Coffee House, we sat in the section marked 'Families Only'. I ordered a Coke for her and went to greet my friends. They were not very complimentary about Georgine. Said my Sikh journalist friend: 'From the way you described her, I thought you had picked up a Marilyn Monroe. Nice fat boobs and bum though!'

'She's no Noor Jahan,' opined the political expert. 'Like any American schoolgirl. Must have a nice pussy. But you must be madder than I thought; you try any tricks with that one, you will be in for seven years' rigorous imprisonment.'

Ugly, vulgar words. I rejoined Georgine. 'What did they have to say about your girl-friend?' she asked.

'Girlfriend? Oh, you mean you?' I replied, pretending to have been taken by surprise. 'They said you were very beautiful.'

'Liar! I bet you a hundred dollars they said, "What are you doin' with a lil' girl like that? Foolin' around with anyone under seventeen can land you in a jail." How 'bout that for a guess?'

'Wrong, wrong, wrong,' I protested vehemently. I could see she was happy.

This time she put my fee in an envelope and gave it to me with 'Thanks a whole lot.'

That evening I was by turns exhilarated and conscience-stricken. In my confusion I rang her up without having anything to say to her. Her uncle picked up the phone. 'You must not let Georgine make a nuisance of herself,' he said, 'and let me have your bill for the time she's been with you.' He put down the receiver without asking me why I had called. But I was excited to know that Georgine had paid me without telling her uncle.

I decided to use the information at an appropriate moment. Meanwhile I became bolder in my compliments. Since she changed her hairstyle every day, I got many opportunities to say things that would please her. One day she dressed herself in a bright red sari. It did not suit her, nor did she know how a woman in a sari should walk—like most Caucasians, she had a masculine stride. I said 'How charming'—and she replied: 'Oh thank you, I thought you'd sort of like to see me in your native costume.' I explained that the sari was not native to the Punjab and that a salwar-kameez would look even nicer on her. 'O great!' she exclaimed. 'I must have these thingees at once.' I took her to a tailor and while she was choosing the material, I told him in Punjabi to send the finished products with the bill, to me. Georgine could not make up her mind. What she liked best, she said, was too expensive for her. So she settled for second best. I spoke to the tailor (again in Punjabi) to use the material of her first choice.

'You think it will look nice on me?' she asked me when we were in the car.

'I am sure it will. We have a word in our language—*jamazebi*—which means, the ability to fit into any clothes. I think you will look nice in anything you wear.' (Far from being *jamazeb*, because of her large bosom and broad hips, Georgine had difficulty in fitting into readymade clothes.) 'You are nuts,' she said dismissing the compliment. 'I know none of the nice things you say are true, but I like you sayin' them. So don't stop, O-Kay?'

Getting her into my apartment was easy. Two days after she had been measured, I offered to drive her around in my own car. When I went to pick her up, I said as casually as I could, 'Your things have been delivered to my apartment. Would you like to pick them up before we go sightseeing?'

'O-Kay.'

She looked around admiringly at my books and pictures. 'Nice, comfy pad,' she remarked.

'Thank you. Do sit down.'

She took off her shoes, bounced onto the settee and crossed her legs. 'Nunc! What you starin' at?'

I quoted Ghalib, first in Urdu and then translated it for her: 'She has come to my house. Sometimes I look at her, sometimes I look at my house.'

'That means you're pleased to have me here. Where are my thingees?'

I brought the bundle and untied it. 'I didn't order that one; it was too expensive, you remember? That old tailor is tryin' to rob me. All you Indians try to fleece us Americans. You think we're a bunch of suckers, don't you?'

'He's not charging you any more for this material. He knew you liked it better, so he's made it just for you.'

She was nonplussed. 'I am sorry. That's very nice of him. And this?' she asked, opening out a sequined dupatta, 'It is very pretty, but I didn't ask for this.'

'That goes with the other things. Nothing extra.'

She draped it over her head and looked around for a mirror. 'Where can I try them on?' she asked, taking the bundle under her arm. I showed her to my bedroom. I was left alone for some time. I poured myself a whisky and gulped it down neat. I moved from the chair to the sofa.

Georgine came out in Punjabi clothes.
The dupatta was like a small white cloud
studded with stars haloing her red hair, face
and shoulders. The clothes fitted her. It
seemed as if she were formed to wear Punjabi
clothes. 'How's that?' she asked pirouetting
on her toes.

'Very becoming! Much nicer than
anything you've worn.'

'Thank you, I sort of like it too.'

She came and sat beside me on the sofa.
She opened her handbag, 'How much does
he want for this?'

My voice stuck in my throat, I forced it
out. 'Nothing. Allow me the privilege of
making this a present. Please!'

'Thank you and all that. But I know you
can't afford it.'

'Yes I can; and it'll make me very happy.'

'Okay, if it'll make you happy.' She turned
around and gave me a quick kiss on my
beard, 'Thank you, pop.'

The kiss paralysed my tongue. After a
while I was able to say: 'And I owe you
money. You paid me for the outings out of
your own money, didn't you?'

'How do you know?'

'I rang up your uncle.'

She turned scarlet. 'That was a dumb thing to do! What did he say?'

I took her hand in mine. 'Don't worry. I did not tell him you had paid me. Now I can earn a double fee.'

'You cunning ole Oriental!' she laughed. 'I'm relieved to know my ole uncle doesn't know.'

'Why didn't you tell him?'

'I dunno.'

The initiative was now mine. 'Maybe you wanted to be with me without his knowing.'

'Maybe,' she replied tossing back her hair.

Any experienced lecher knows that one should not waste words with a teenager because when it comes to real business she gets tongue-tied or can only say 'No.' It is best to talk to her body with your hands. That excites her to a state of speechless acceptance. I ran my fingers up and down her lower arm. She watched them till goose pimples came up. Thereafter, all I had to do was to put my arm around her waist, draw her towards me and smother her lips, eyes, nose,

ears and neck with kisses. She moaned
helplessly. I slipped my hand under her
kameez and played with her taut nipples.
Then I undid her pyjama cord and slipped
my fingers between her damp thighs. A little
gentle ministration with my hand made her
convulse and she climaxed groaning 'O God!
O God!' She lay still like a human-sized
rubber doll. I put my hand on her bosom. She
slapped it and pushed it away. She picked up
her clothes and went to the bedroom. She
came back in her jeans, tossed the bundle of
salwar-kameez and sequined dupatta on the
settee and strode out of the apartment.

That was the last I saw of Georgine.

And she was the last customer Carlyle
put my way. I do not know whether what I
had done had amounted to having carnal
knowledge of a girl below the age of consent.
But for many long days and nights, I pondered
over the words in the *Mahabharata*: 'As two
pieces of wood floating on the ocean come
together at one time and are again separated,
even such is the union of living creatures in
this world.'